THE GUTTER AND THE GHETTO

THE GUTTER AND THE GHETTO

by Don Wilkerson
with Herm Weiskopf

WORD BOOKS, PUBLISHER

WACO, TEXAS   39539   LONDON, ENGLAND

THE GUTTER AND THE GHETTO

Library of Congress Catalog Card Number: 70-91938

Printed in the United States of America

First Printing—October 1969
Second Printing—October 1970
Third Printing—May 1971

contents

one /...
···/ in the beginning

WHEN I THINK BACK to how it all began, I realize that the starting point was the first day of March in 1958. At that time I was a freshman at what was then called Eastern Bible Institute (it is now known as Northeast Bible College) in Green Lane, Pennsylvania, some 40 miles outside of Philadelphia. As I was walking across the campus that day, I heard someone calling me. I turned around and saw a girl running toward me and as she came closer I saw that she was waving a newspaper.

"Did you hear what happened to your brother?" she asked breathlessly when she had caught up with me. This was Nanny Dann, a student at the school and a member of my brother Dave's church in Philipsburg, Pennsylvania. As she held out the newspaper—it was a copy of the *New York Daily News*—I saw that half of the front page was covered with a picture of Dave. There seemed to be a bit of a frightened look on Dave's face and the Bible, which he was holding above his head, seemed to be hovering there too large to be real, like a huge weight that he was struggling to keep aloft. My first reaction was to laugh ever so slightly.

"Don't you see what happened?" Nanny chided me. "Dave was thrown out of a courtroom in New York City. Here," she said as she thrust the newspaper into my hands, "read it for yourself."

When I finished reading the article I thought to myself, "Well, this time Dave has gone too far with one of his projects. He'll never live this one down." After having read the news-

7

paper account, though, I still didn't know much about the situation. The story told of Dave's having taken an interest in a group of youngsters who were on trial for murder, of his having driven 350 miles from Philipsburg to Manhattan, and of his having been thrown out of the courtroom when he had tried to talk to the judge. Still, I had no idea what had motivated Dave. One thing I did know was that I was not going to become involved in this latest of Dave's far-out ventures, whatever it was. How wrong I was. Dave's courtroom episode, it turned out, led to the founding of Teen Challenge, and the furtherance of this ministry has become my life's work.

Teen Challenge, founded back in 1960 by Dave, was christened Teen-Age Evangelism. During its infancy its goal was to help the teenagers in New York City. Many times when these youngsters got into trouble and reached up for help the adult world stepped on their fingers. Penal authorities often felt that this was the best way to deal with these teenagers, whom they preferred to cast into one big barrel and brand with the same insignia: "punks." The ambivalence that was created was predictable. Young people who were punished so indiscriminately and indiscreetly returned to society not with a chastened or renewed spirit, but rather with a deeper hatred and a more frustrated appraisal of life than before.

Dave was motivated to try to minister to these teenagers in February of 1958 when, while leafing through a copy of *Life* magazine, he came across a picture of seven youths who had been arraigned in the fatal stabbing of a 15-year-old boy named Michael Farmer, a polio victim, at High Bridge Park in Manhattan. Dave glanced at the photographs and the accompanying story, then turned the page. "Punks," he thought to himself. Then came other thoughts. "Who is going to help these boys? Are they just going to be shunted off to prison to rot away? Does anyone care what happens to them?"

There didn't seem to be a thing he could do to aid these youngsters. Still, those questions he had asked himself nagged at him so much that he finally set out for New York to see what he could do. His fervent desire to be helpful soon got him into water that was hot enough to have scalded a man of lesser faith.

After considerable difficulty, Dave got into the courtroom where the boys were on trial on February 28, 1958. His first objective was to speak with Judge Irwin D. Davidson when the day's session was over to see if he could obtain permission to talk to the boys. When the judge announced a recess for the day, Dave went forward as quickly as possible. It was a move that was misinterpreted by the courtroom guards, who had been alerted that there had been threats on the judge's life and that someone might try to attack him. Dave was not exactly pounced upon by the guards, but Judge Davidson did order them to have him removed from the courtroom. A few minutes later, the members of the press crowded around him and he was given a chance to explain his presence at the trial. Photographers, sensing a good picture, asked Dave to pose with his Bible held high in the air, then snapped photographs of him that were soon to be spread across the pages of New York newspapers.

Some people were understanding. Many were not, thinking that Dave had made a fool of himself, a fate they felt should never befall any right-thinking man, especially a minister. Somehow, Dave not only survived the testing days that followed, but actually went back to Manhattan several weeks later. It was then that the Lord began to show Dave that He definitely had a work for him to do in New York City. First of all, He unveiled the reason for the courtroom incident.

It came on the night that Dave and a friend of his from Philipsburg drove to New York again and became lost in the city traffic. Dave got out of the car to find someone from whom to ask directions. A group of teenagers spotted Dave and, much to his surprise, called him "Preacher Davie." They explained that they had seen his picture in the papers and it soon became clear that they felt he was on their side because of the way he had stormed across the courtroom to intercede on behalf of the teenagers who were on trial. These youngsters on the street corner that night not only identified Dave, they identified *with* him.

What a few weeks earlier had been the most humiliating incident in Dave's life was turned into a victory. With the aid of these youngsters, he gained access to the inner circle of the lives of these teenagers, their orgies and gangs, their frenzy and rebellion, their drugs and their torment. He began to find out what it was like to be a kid who was unwanted by his parents, who was unable to find the help he needed at school and in his neighborhood, who felt lost in the vastness of tenement houses and a world without love. To this day, we sometimes wonder what would have happened had Dave not made his courtroom scene and if he had not, after much prayer, returned to Manhattan and become lost. There are too many imponderables, but we are certain that the main ingredient which lay between his two visits to New York—much prayer—had been of incalculable help. We have never ceased to believe this and, as a consequence, have made abundant prayer the cornerstone of our work. Too often and too miraculously we have seen God provide answers when, after failing to accomplish something despite our utmost efforts, we have taken the matter to Him in prayer.

Dave made frequent trips to Manhattan to work among the young people with whom he had come into contact and, within eighteen months after his first trip to the courtroom, he was formulating plans to undertake this as a full-time ministry. During my third and final year in Bible school I received a letter from Dave telling me that he had set up a headquarters for his new work on Staten Island. In the letter he expressed his burden for this work and told me of his need for fellow-workers. He simply laid before me the challenge to join him as soon as I graduated.

Those were difficult days for our family. Dad had passed away a few months earlier. I came home from school on weekends and teamed up with Mom to take over the pastorate of my father's church in Scranton, Pennsylvania, for a few months until the people there were able to find a new minister. Mom was concerned about the church but also about Dave and his latest move. One night, she called to talk about these things and about what we should do. I was apprehensive about something I felt she might ask and, sure enough, she asked me: "Are you going to go to New York to join Dave?" This was precisely the question I had been wrestling with for weeks.

I knew that Mom would have liked for me to have helped

carry on Dad's ministry in Scranton. Some members of the congregation had expressed a desire for Mom to stay on, but she soon realized that there was too much work there for her and that she would need my help to make a go of it. It hurt me to tell her that I wasn't going to join forces with her, especially since I couldn't give her any good reason why I had decided to go with Dave. Mom did her best in Scranton for as long as she was able to, then had to admit that it was too strenuous a job for her to take on alone. As soon as the church was able to get a full-time pastor, Mom left Scranton to join Dave, serving officially as his secretary and unofficially—and much more vitally—as his advisor on spiritual matters.

One of the most persistent thoughts throughout my adolescent and teenage life had been that I wanted to be used by the Lord. Actually, this became more than a mere thought. As a pastor's son, I had become intimately involved with church work at an early age and had felt that this was the sort of labor that the Lord was preparing me for. From my early teens on, I harbored the belief that I would someday take up the pastorate of a church and that this would be my permanent work. I sincerely feel that the only reason I did not fulfill this ambition was because it was transcended by one that was more important, namely, a fervent desire to be used by the Lord wherever He called me, not merely where I wanted to go.

It was when Dave wrote to me during my final year in Bible school that I realized the depth of such a simple-sounding phrase as "being used by the Lord." I had told people for years that this was my desire, and I had kept repeating it, sensing that it was both pleasant to my ear and apparently to those of my listeners. But when Dave challenged me to join him in his work I discovered that I had been using words that carried more weight than I had ever realized.

I had many misgivings about teaming up with Dave. For one thing, I didn't know specifically what sort of work he was becoming involved in except that he was trying to help teenagers in New York. It was hard for me to convince myself that the Lord wanted me to work among those youngsters rather than among those in any other community. Still another little something that caused me to have doubts about working for Dave was the size of the operating budget for his ministry; it could hardly even have been described as a shoestring budget, for, at best, this shoestring must have been broken in half a dozen places and knotted back together.

Was something so tenuous as this the proper place for me to begin my own ministry, one that I had been dreaming about for so long, one that I felt held forth so much promise? Would it be right working for my brother? Even more important, was this project of Dave's really God-inspired or had my over-zealous brother merely hatched an idea that would soon pass away? I recalled that my father, when he had first learned of Dave's intentions concerning this work, had been strongly opposed.

Had I had my own way, I believe that I would have by-passed Dave's request and tried to establish myself in a small church in some peaceful hamlet. Rejecting Dave's invitation, however, was something I felt I did not have the liberty to do without the Lord's permission.

When the time came for me to make my decision, I was surprised to find that the Lord was leading me toward Dave instead of away from him. I decided that if that was where the Lord wanted to use me, then that was where I would go. Thus it was that in the spring of 1961, after I had graduated, I joined Mom and Dave at their meager headquarters on Staten Island, just a ferryboat ride across the bay from Manhattan.

For me, Manhattan was not Fun City or a town filled with excitement. I spent little time in Manhattan. Our office, such as it was, was located in the town of Castleton Corners on Victory Boulevard. Space was at such a premium that we had to make certain the three of us didn't wind up in the same room at the same time, for we might have become hopelessly wedged together. The outer office was large enough for a desk, a chair for Mom to sit in, and not much else. Down the hall a few paces was Dave's office, fully equipped with desk, chair, and a cot, on which he spent many a night—a lot of them sleepless. Behind Dave's office was my residence, otherwise known as the shipping room. My modern working equipment included miles of string, buckets of glue, scissors, address labels, rubber stamps to imprint our name on the tracts we handed out, and yards and yards and yards of brown wrapping paper.

My job was that of an errand boy and, boy, did I run errands! I ran to the post office to mail stacks of letters containing information about our work in the hope that people would recognize us, take an interest, and contribute to our support. I ran to one store to get glue and string. To another store I ran for sandwiches and to yet another for pencils. Trips to the bank were few and far between; our budget was infinitesimal.

It was quite a letdown. There I was, an ordained minister wrapping packages, scurrying to the bank before it closed so I could cash a check for three dollars so we could buy some food to eat that night. It wasn't easy for Mom, either. Her life was undergoing quite an adjustment and not even the rehabilitating hours of work would keep her from being aware of the birth pangs of this new—and almost destitute ministry.

Instead of being able to preach impassioned sermons from a pulpit, my personal ministry was limited to an occasional chat with a teenager and the passing out of tracts which told of Christ and of our work. One of the gimmicks we came up with as we sought new ways of getting through to the youngsters was what we called the Flip-Top Box. In size it was similar to the flip-top cigarette boxes; in content, though, our boxes were quite different, for they were filled with an assortment of tracts which we hoped the kids would read. We also had what we labeled Truth Capsules. These were plastic capsules that resembled medicine vials and, like our Flip-Top Boxes, were filled with tracts. Sometimes when we were riding in a car and would see a cluster of youngsters we used to throw batches of Flip-Top Boxes and Truth Capsules at them. These were attention-getting devices which worked very well in helping to pave the way for Dave, who began holding meetings with assorted groups and with gangs in the metropolitan area.

My role in the ministry was a much less active one than Dave's, and it was a few months before I was able to undertake a project of my own. This involved a trip to a small town in upstate New York about twenty miles from Elmira, where a local congregation had written to Dave requesting someone to come and conduct a series of meetings for the young people. Dave was too tied up to make the trip himself, so he delegated the assignment to me.

Some friends of mine drove me up there. When they left they kidded and said they felt sorry for me and regretted leaving me in this countrified little town. Then when I got my first glimpse of the church I almost shouted out, "Hurray, the place is abandoned. I can go back home." Prayer seemed to be about the only thing keeping the building from tumbling down. No one had been praying about the lawn, obviously, for it was overgrown to jungle-like proportions. Just as I had convinced myself that the place really was deserted and that I could return home, the door of the parsonage opened and out came an elderly man. He walked over to where I was standing, stretched out his hand and said, "Brother Don, praise the Lord. So glad you agreed to come. I'm sure the Lord will bless you for it."

"Yes," I replied as I fumbled for words. "It's—ah—good to be here." To cover my embarrassment, I tried to think of something else to say and blurted out a stupid question: "Is this the—ah—church where I'll be speaking?"

"Yes, indeed," he said. "Come take a look at it before I take you to your room. Built most of it myself, with a little help from the congregation, naturally."

I had to restrain myself from saying that it was a shame there hadn't been an architect in the congregation. Just a few moments in this man's presence, though, was all that was needed to become aware of his sincerity and his humility. As we looked around the church I could sense that he was proud of this structure and I somehow felt that he had reason to be. The parsonage was built in the same style as the church—early American hodgepodge. As I looked around the parsonage, however, my respect for the pastor deepened, sensing as I did that this was a man who truly loved God. He had used the best materials he had to build the house of God and had constructed his own home from the leftovers.

During my stay up there I lived with the pastor, who was a widower. The furnishings were antiquated and the house had long ago lost its orderliness. Modern conveniences were nonexistent. Water had to be boiled on the big kitchen stove, which also served as the central heating system. A path and a flashlight led to the outhouse.

Surprisingly, the meetings went very well. Those country folk didn't have the problems of their counterparts in New York, but they were concerned about the conditions of youngsters there and they were filled with questions about what they could do to help and how they could do it. At last, I felt that I was doing something worthwhile, that I was making people aware of the needs of others.

The first few days, though, were a struggle. Privacy in the parsonage was at a premium. Most of the studying I had to do in preparing my messages had to be done at one end of the kitchen while the pastor cooked and washed dishes at the other end. The aroma of his cooking hardly affected my concentration, but his method of washing dishes was more than I could take sitting down. He never bothered to heat water for the task. Instead, he merely placed the dishes in a tub of cold water, dumped in a little detergent and gave the dishes a once-over-lightly swishing with a cloth.

After watching this ritual a few times I decided something had to be done. "I ought to be ashamed," I said to the pastor one night. "There I sit, studying away and not even helping you with the dishes."

"That's all right," he said kindly. "I want you to spend all your spare time on your messages. Besides, I'm used to doing dishes. You go right on studying."

"No, I insist," I said. It seemed to me that my voice conveyed more panic than brotherliness, though. Trying to mount a convincing argument, I said, "I really do need some exercise; I don't get much in the City." Before he could argue, I had rolled up my shirt sleeves and had begun a dish-washing job that would have left Mom speechless. Every night from then on I did the dishes the same way, boiling a huge pot of water and then vigorously scrubbing the dishes in the hope that I could get rid of the germs that I felt certain were gathering for a massive attack on our digestive systems. As much as I disliked washing dishes, this routine was much easier to get used to than were the trips to the outhouse, which always seemed to turn into adventuresome forays on which I could depend on encountering at least one or two snakes.

The meetings I was conducting at the church continued to go well, but I was counting the days until my friends would return to take me back home. My week was almost over when I was faced with an unexpected dilemma: I was invited by the church to stay on for another week of meetings. This was a real testing of my faith. Did I have faith enough to do the dishes every night for another week? Was my faith sufficient to uphold me as I tiptoed around the numerous snakes who always seemed to try to intercept me as I made my way to the outhouse?

First I prayed about the matter and then I told the people that, yes, I would stay on for another week. Then I began counting the days all over again.

It was good to get back to Staten Island after the second week of meetings and it wasn't long before I became involved in the making of a movie with Dave and Ralphie Geigle, the first drug addict to come to the Lord under my brother's ministry. We rented a 16-mm camera and lights from a store in Manhattan and then set out to make like Cecil B. DeMille. Our budget for the movie was right up there in the five-figure bracket: $102.97. It was a good thing that our hopes were considerably higher than our bank balance, and it was with much determination, if little skill, that we plunged into film making.

The key man was Ralphie. He was going to play the part of a drug addict in the film. And he was going to help us to get some of the rarest film footage extant by arranging for us to come to a rooftop drug party where addicts would let us photograph them as they actually shot drugs into their veins with hypodermic needles.

Came the big day for the rooftop scene and the three of us were all prepared. Ralphie led us to the roof of a building in the South Williamsburg section of Brooklyn on South Second Street. Dave poised his camera and took pictures of the youngsters as they heated their heroin to liquefy it and then as they filled up their needles so they could inject themselves. I held the lights as steady as I could.

Then, just as one of the addicts plunged a needle into his arm, Dave did a fadeout, only it wasn't the camera fading out—it was Dave. He passed out cold. For a few frightening minutes I didn't know what to do. A strange city and even stranger people. My brother unconscious way up on a rooftop. One thing I knew I couldn't do was to call the police. If I had, Dave's picture would again have been fodder for newspapers everywhere and this time the stories would have been even more damning, for he would have had a hard time explaining away his presence at a rooftop drugfest.

After what seemed like an eon, Dave snapped out of it. I felt relieved. But when Dave stood up and began to cry, I didn't know what to think. Then he unburdened himself to me and said that because of what had happened to him he now felt broken before the Lord. He felt that God had used his weakness so that he might arise in His strength.

Right there on top of that building we prayed for the Lord to help us to do something meaningful for drug addicts and to make us willing to labor as long and as hard as necessary. This was the instant when God gave us a real glimpse of the tragic plight of the drug addict and put it on our hearts to dedicate our lives to helping these people. When we finished our prayers we both felt revitalized.

In a sense, we had to go all the way *up* to a rooftop so that we could get *down* on our knees. Now, with our sights set higher, with our vision broader, and with our compassion more heartfelt, we were prepared to get busy.

It was a rather crude film that we finally put together. Nevertheless, it had its virtues. It got into the inner workings of drug addiction as perhaps no other movie had done up to that time and thus was able to portray some of the seriousness and tragedy of the drug problem. When the film was completed it became my task to go on tour with it in an effort to make our new type of work known to the public and to raise funds. By the time my travels were over, the odometer on my station wagon had registered more than twenty thousand miles.

Road maps were my constant front-seat companions for the next eight months. Pennsylvania, Maryland, Virginia, North Carolina, South Carolina—the states rushed by and soon the

Florida sun beckoned. One of my early stops was in Lake Worth, Florida, where an uncle of mine—Reverend John Wilkerson—pastored a church. I showed the movie there and during the next two months pretty well covered the length and breadth of the state, stopping off at churches in Fort Pierce, Fort Myers, Key West, and dozens of smaller communities like Okeechobee.

When I had left on this trip my itinerary was fairly extensive but as I travelled on and on through Florida and then into the Carolinas I kept getting letters from Dave saying that he had received word from another church that was interested in seeing the film. It was nice to get all this mail from Dave, especially since we couldn't afford to keep calling each other. To be truthful, however, I wasn't nearly as anxious about checking into a motel and looking for a letter from him as I was about receiving one from someone else. Her name was Cindy.

We had met at Bible school and our courtship had reached the stage where we were considering marriage. Letters from Cindy, who had graduated and was now living at home in Plainfield, Vermont, took the drudgery out of my days. Not only did I read and reread them when they first came, I saved them from the day I left home, kept them in a bundle with a rubber band around them, and spent many an hour reading them all again and again.

I was more than pleased with the response of the people to the film and with the donations that they made to our work. I knew that I was getting weary, yet the challenge in each town was always new, for people were just learning about our ministry and it was refreshing to see their interest and their concern. It was a difficult trip, though. Every day a new town, a new church, new people—and a new motel room. Everything started to look the same and food lost its savor.

On a trip such as this—at least for someone as young and inexperienced at travelling as I was—the time passed slowly. I became increasingly restless. At best, I felt that I was serving the Lord in some roundabout fashion. My desire was to plunge into a more active ministry, but I knew that Mom and Dave would not be able to keep things going back in New York if

I didn't send back the money contributed by those who viewed our movie.

One Sunday night near the end of my journey I was at a church in the western part of Michigan. On Wednesday I was supposed to be in Montreal with the movie. Well, after I finished up my last showing in Michigan, I climbed into my station wagon, drove off into the night and just happened to be headed in the direction of—well, to be truthful—Plainfield, Vermont.

Despite the success of my trip, I returned to Staten Island more discouraged than encouraged. I told Dave, "I don't want to *talk* about the work. I want to *do* the work." This was early in 1962 and things weren't progressing too well at Teen Challenge. Dave sat me down and told me that it might be best if I took over the pastorate of a church somewhere. He felt that such a job would give me a chance to gain some experience and maturity. I agreed, and when I learned of an opening at a church in Barre, Vermont, just a few miles from where Cindy lived, I knew that my search for a pastorate was over.

two /...
···/ the faithful five
/ and the surfside chapel

I CALLED DAVE from Barre to break the news that I had accepted the job there. For a few seconds there was no response from Dave. I thought we had been cut off, so I said, "Dave, are you still there?"

"How many members, Don?"

"Six."

Pause.

"How much are they going to pay you?"

"Nothing."

Long pause.

"Are you sure you know what you're doing?"

My only explanation to Dave was that I hadn't even hesitated about saying yes in spite of these drawbacks. I somehow sensed that this was where the Lord wanted me.

I didn't draw any salary from the church, but the members did provide me with an apartment and they did pay for the telephone there. Aside from that, I had to fend for myself as best I could, and that meant taking an outside job. Money and I were strangers one to the other, but at this particular time I knew that there was a need for some cash. Cindy and I were going to be married on May 31, less than three months hence.

My apartment, on the second floor of a house owned by one of the local women, was unfurnished except for an old rollaway. Cindy had a job as a secretary with an insurance company in nearby Montpelier and I got a job as a guide at the huge granite quarries in Barre, home of the Rock of Ages, the company that makes tombstones and monuments. Finances

20

being what they were, Cindy and I revised our honeymoon plans, taking the only sort of honeymoon we had known we would ever be able to afford: a weekend in Maine.

For our Sunday morning services we sometimes had as many as three dozen people in our church. On Sunday evenings and at our midweek services we could always count on five people—no more, no less. Our Faithful Five consisted of four elderly women and the gentleman who was the only male member of our congregation. He worked hard all day long and somewhere near the middle of our night's program I could rely on his dozing off. Sometimes he would tell me, "My, those Wednesday night services certainly are refreshing." I could only say, "Yes, I suppose they are."

I had gone to Barre in quest of maturity and experience and, one way or the other, I was getting what I had wanted. More trying than anything else was the difficulty that Cindy had after she became pregnant. She experienced much sickness and pain and we became increasingly concerned. Added to this was a worsening of our financial situation, for with the advent of winter all the guides at the quarries were laid off until springtime. Jobs were at a premium and a newcomer to the area like me didn't stand much of a chance.

Ever hear of a son-in-law who looked forward to seeing his mother-in-law every day of the week? I was guilty of this out-of-character behavior, but there was method to my madness: after a month or so without employment, our cupboard was bare, a condition that did not exist at my mother-in-law's home. Besides, Mrs. Hudson was a warm-hearted woman who gladly fed us whenever we would pop in. We made the eight-mile drive over the hill on the slightest pretext and, oddly, always arrived at her home around mealtime. We thanked God that we were able to go there so often knowing that we were always welcome and that even if we told her, "We just came to say hello," that she would insist upon our having a meal, complete with seconds and dessert. Then, as we would be leaving, she would wink at us and say, "Thanks so much for stopping by to say hello."

One day during this period of my unemployment as I was pacing around the apartment, too restless to take care of the household chores such as doing the dishes and making the bed, I decided that what I needed to do more than anything else was to pray. I went into the bedroom, got down on my knees and began praying. A few minutes later, I heard the door to the apartment open. I kept on praying, for I recognized that the voices of those who had entered were those of Cindy and her sister. (I didn't know it at that moment, but Cindy had become ill that day and had fainted while at work; her sister was bringing her home.) Well, when my sister-in-law saw me in the bedroom and noticed the unmade bed she thought that I had been taking a nap. Biting off her words, she said to Cindy, "Isn't that something. You're so sick you can hardly stand, and he's at home sleeping."

Things kept getting worse instead of better. Cindy was in about the seventh month of her pregnancy when, in accordance with her company's rules, she was not permitted to work any longer. She was able to collect unemployment compensation, but it really hurt our pride to have to accept those checks. I was embarrassed about our financial position, frustrated by my failure to obtain a job and, above all, more bewildered than I had been in all my life.

Although the idea seemed somewhat ludicrous at the time, I remember straining to make myself realize that this logjam of difficulties was not without merit and that it was somehow going to help to mature me. Try as I might to adopt a grateful attitude toward the plight in which I found myself, though, it was hard to see how these testings were going to make me stand taller. Little by little, I began to realize that life in the adult world was far more demanding than I had imagined. I almost began pining for those years of simplicity which were now behind me, when even the most calamitous events in life—a spanking from Dad, striking out with the bases loaded, getting a poor grade in my school work—would be forgotten in a day or two.

Getting a job as a clerk in a grocery store alleviated the pressures brought to bear by our creditors, and trips to my mother-in-law's home alleviated the pangs in our stomachs. Things were beginning to look up a bit. On Wednesday nights I would gaze out at my appreciative audience—my Faithful

Five—and then I would look over at Cindy and we would share a smile.

Our smiles were turned to tears in January when Cindy was rushed to the hospital one morning. A few hours later the doctor came to me as I was seated in the hospital waiting room. "Your wife is fine, but the baby was stillborn," he said.

It wasn't long after that day that I received a letter from Dave. He must have had a good concept of the troubled days through which we had passed, for his letter was overflowing with encouragement and warmth. One paragraph stood out in glaring prominence: "Don," it read, "the work has grown tremendously in the past several months and I need your assistance. I need someone who not only understands the nature of this work, but someone I can completely trust and depend upon. The board of directors are aware of this need and I'm sure will take my recommendation. It won't be easy on you and Cindy, but the challenge is here waiting for you to accept it."

I couldn't wait to break the news to Cindy. She was preparing lunch. "Cindy," it was hard to keep the joy I felt out of my voice, "how would you like to live in New York City?" I wasn't sure what her response would be to Dave's offer because she didn't particularly like any city, let alone one of the largest of the world.

"I'm not worried about having to live in New York, Don," she said, "but don't you think we'd be taking the easy way out of our situation here?"

Well, I wasn't expecting that sort of response at all. Maybe I was looking for a way out, leaving my small congregation in the lurch. I was downright confused.

"Well, honey, we'd better pray about this," I said. "Dave will be expecting an answer soon. I don't like leaving the church with such a small membership, but I think that the Lord might want us elsewhere."

No sooner had I finished talking than Cindy began laughing.

"What's so funny?" I asked.

"I was just thinking," Cindy said when she had finished laughing, "about who in the world would ever accept the pastorate if you left."

I had to laugh, too, knowing that the size of the congregation and the pay would not attract a lot of candidates. Then,
realizing that I had accepted the job in spite of those conditions,
I laughed some more.

When we had both settled down, I said, "You know something, honey, I just had a terrible thought: maybe Dave is
asking us to come because he feels sorry for us. You know how
Dave is."

"I've had the same suspicion," Cindy told me. "But I know
who would really know whether you are needed or not."

I knew who, too: Mom.

"I'll call her right now," I said.

"Mom," I said, "I guess you know that Dave wrote and
asked me to come back to help. What I want to know is—and
please be honest with me—does Dave *really* need me?"

"Well, Don, as far as I know, he does need you. There isn't
enough staff now to handle the boys who are coming in and he
needs someone who can take over the complete program while
he's gone."

"Thanks, Mom. That relieves me. I still haven't made up
my mind what to do, but now that I know Dave really needs
me I'll be able to come up with an answer soon."

I still wasn't satisfied that rejoining Dave was what the
Lord wanted me to do. The more I prayed about the situation
the more He seemed to be telling me that it would be proper
for me to leave if a new minister could be found quickly for
the church. That seemed like an impossibility. Within a few
days, however, a visiting minister told me about a young pastor
who was looking for a small church he could take over. It just
so happened that I knew of a church like that—and we were as
good as gone.

Almost exactly a year to the day I had left Dave, I returned. It was comforting to have Cindy in the car beside me as
we drove to Dave's new headquarters in Brooklyn for that very
first time. This was to be my first experience driving in big-
city traffic and I had tried to steel myself for it. Nevertheless,
as the traffic got heavier and the buildings taller and the car
horns louder, I could feel myself getting tense. What made the
driving even more difficult was that I had a hard time keeping

my eyes off the startling sights that passed in profusion: buildings gutted by fire, broken windows everywhere, streets littered with debris, squalor screaming from every corner—and people walking amid this clutter, people who were totally oblivious to it all. What kind of a place was this, I asked myself. I could see that this area where Dave had been called to minister was in the mouth of the serpent. Now I could understand why he had advised me to take a pastorate and gain some maturity before plunging into this sort of work.

By this time—it was now the spring of 1963—Dave had been able to raise enough funds to purchase a building on Clinton Avenue in Brooklyn. When we finally got to Clinton Avenue we kept looking for No. 416, which was the address Dave had given to us.

"There it is, Don," Cindy almost shouted when she spotted 416 at long last. "After all we just saw, I didn't expect it to be so nice."

It certainly was a lot better than most of the places we had seen in the area, for 416 was a four-story red brick colonial house nestled between two aparment buildings. Outside, there was a sign identifying 416 as the Teen Challenge Center. Inside, we had a warm reunion with Dave and, as he told us about the staggering number of things that had been taking place since we had left and about the enlarged scope of the ministry, I began to appreciate that I was, indeed, needed.

The small salary I was to receive never would have been sufficient for us to rent a place of our own, so Mom suggested that we move in with her. She still lived on Staten Island, as did Dave and his family. Together, we commuted to work, usually by car. Sometimes, though, we took the deluxe route to work: a two-block walk from the house to the bus stop, a ride to the ferry, a briny trip across the channel, a bone-crunching ride aboard a subway, a change to another subway and then, to top it all off, another short walk. That brought us to 416, which was how we all referred to our headquarters.

My ministry was to be on Coney Island. Dave wanted to set up a chapel near the boardwalk. The many booths already lined up side by side attracted the attention of thousands of people. Dave's idea was to reach these same people with good gospel singing, down-to-earth salvation messages and soul-searching tracts. It was my job to head this ministry. I wasn't at all sure that I would be capable of handling such a task, but Dave was aware of my qualms and promised to go along with me the first night to help get things started. I appreciated his understanding.

That first night, though, was like spending a year in a pressure cooker. Dave had opened the program and as I watched him I thought to myself, "I'll never be able to be at ease in front of such a crowd. Dave was cut out for this kind of work; I wasn't." When Dave called on me to take over the meeting, my knees rattled and my stomach felt as if I had swallowed a rock. I recall praying quickly, "Lord, You'll have to help me. I can't do it alone." When I opened my mouth to speak I was fearfu! that nothing would come out. Words did manage to struggle forth, slowly at first and then at a faster and faster tempo. By the end of the evening I felt that I was in command of the situation and the first chance I had to take a breather I thanked the Lord for what He had accomplished.

Our booth was nothing more than a couple of collapsible walls. People could look right in and they could also come right in and seat themselves on the fifty or so folding chairs that we set up each night. Across the street from where we were located there was a bar where a lot of homosexuals gathered. When they heard our program on opening night, a good many were curious enough to come over and see what was going on. The owner came over to us too and, wagging a finger in our faces, predicted, "You'll never last."

Well, we lasted three years, by which time our friend from across the street was long out of business, one of many who closed up as Coney Island economy took a nosedive.

Our program was basically the same night after night. We would start at about 8 o'clock and for the first half hour or so we would sing hymns and have some of our workers present testimonies concerning their Christian faith. Then I would give a brief devotional and would invite people to come in. Loud-speakers carried our words and songs beyond our immediate area with excellent results.

We had many blessings during our years at the Surfside

Chapel. One night, we were getting ready to close up when a big, inquisitive-looking Negro man came over to our booth. It was plain to see that he was curious about what was going on. But let him tell his own story:

"I first heard about Teen Challenge when I was in prison. I read a story about how they were setting up a chapel out on Coney Island. I forgot all about that, but while I was in Sing Sing I came to accept the Lord as my Savior. You see, I was in on a burglary charge. Since I was a little child I had problems with the home. I started running away when I was eight years old. When I reached the age of ten or so, they started putting me in reformatories and institutions like that and there's where I learned much more about crime. I went on a binge and the last time I got caught it was a trip to Sing Sing. I didn't have any hope for the future until July 23, 1961. I was thirty-five years old at the time, but that was the day I told Christ I was a sinner and that I was sorry and that I wanted Him to take over my life.

"After I got out of prison it was hard getting situated. I was wandering around Coney Island on the boardwalk and I looked across the street and saw this chapel. Suddenly, I remembered the story that I had read. They were just closing up for the night. I walked across the street to the chapel and someone asked me, 'Are you a Christian?'

"I said, 'Yes, praise the Lord.'

"Pretty soon the group gathered around me and they wanted to hear my testimony, so I told them. I didn't have any place to go so I asked one of them if I could come to Teen Challenge. I was invited to come to the Center and that was how I was accepted into Teen Challenge and got started on my way to dedicating my life to full-time ministry."

three /...
···/ speaking up

L ITTLE BY LITTLE, the work was prospering. It was beautiful
to behold, much like watching the growth of a flower in
slow motion. Gang members and addicts began to respect Dave.
Young people were helped. As others saw or heard about the
fruit of the work they helped to support it financially. Some
even volunteered to assist Dave in this lonely, difficult task.
And the Lord found a way to use me more effectively once I
submitted to Him in joy and hope and forgot my fear and
anxiety. My major stumbling block at first was my fear of
personal evangelism. This was no small problem, for since its
inception the backbone of the work at Teen Challenge has
been its street ministry, its effort to reach people through personal contact and to convince them that we sincerely want to
help them. And it was this very kind of work with which I
had almost no experience.

As long as I had been allowed to do my preaching and
witnessing in a church, I had been in my element. Until I
had come to Teen Challenge, though, my ministry had been
pulpit-oriented. For me there was now a fear of stepping out
of the pulpit and onto the street corner with the same message.
This street ministry was so new, so different, so frightening that
I could not cope with it at first. It was a very real fear, not of
bodily harm, but a fear which, nevertheless, quickens the heart-
beat to a jackhammer pace and which dries the throat. Thus
plagued, I found that the thoughts I felt I could express in
church with some eloquence were now being uttered with
labor, if at all, when I faced people on the street.

Dave recognized my shortcomings and assured me that practice would lead to improvement. I wasn't quite so certain. My ineffectiveness in the street ministry left me in a quandary and caused me to do a lot of thinking. I realized that I had been reared in the pulpit and had been permitted to speak from there from the time I was sixteen years old. My father had let me fill in for him now and then and had so often told me, "Don, you're going to be the next preacher in the family," that I had never before doubted it.

The summers when I had been fourteen, fifteen, and sixteen, I had spent with Dave in Philipsburg and he had let me speak to youth groups. After my last summer with Dave I had gone home to Scranton, where my father taught me how to prepare sermon outlines. By the time I was eighteen I was able to fill in for Dad during just about any church service and was able to converse freely with people within the confines of our church structure. It wasn't until I came to Brooklyn that I found out that I was unable to converse with the man on the street.

To overcome this took prayer. I had to pray for God to relieve me of my personal fears so that I might think first of my desire to be His obedient servant. I had to ask myself if I were willing to submit my will to His and if I were in earnest about wanting to be used by God. Realizing that I wanted to submit and that I wanted to be used, I talked to God about my problem of witnessing to people face to face.

Within a short time I became aware that God had answered my prayers, had removed the doubts and fears, had unloosed my tongue and, beyond that, had given me pleasure in this sort of street-corner evangelism. What a short time before had almost been my undoing was soon transformed into the core of my ministry.

While some people may have more of a knack for street ministry than others, I believe that anyone can be an effective witness if he is truly motivated by a love for God. Those who are not as fluent, or as confident, or as experienced as others simply have to keep at it until they have acquired the ability. To those who shake their heads or shrug their shoulders and claim that they just weren't cut out for this sort of thing, I like to tell these stories about two others who felt the same way. One was a young boy named Thurman; the other was Cindy.

Thurman was a Negro who had come to help us with our street ministry, but when it came time for him to go out and do the work he shook his head.

"I can't do it," he said.

"Why not?" Dave wanted to know.

"I don't have a burden for that kind of work. I can't be of any help if I don't have the burden, can I?"

"Thurman," Dave asked, "what would you do if you *had* a burden?"

"I'd plunge right into the work," he replied. "I'd give of myself to help other people."

"Well, that's just what everyone has to do," Dave explained. "When you start in this street ministry you have to go ahead and do what you would do if you had a burden, and in the process you'll develop one."

Thurman heaved a sigh, consented to give it a try and then plunged into the work. When the day's work had ended, Thurman spoke up: "You know what?" he asked. "I *do* have a burden."

I had to smile, for my case had been much the same. One of the important things to keep in mind is that burdens don't come—poof—out of wishes and thin air. They consist of inner convictions, a desire to be helpful, a willingness to think more about another person's needs than your own fears, and an ability to yield yourself to the Lord's will.

We have frequent pep talks for members of the Teen Challenge staff to help them better understand how to become successful witnesses in our street ministry. Many of the workers admit that they have an uneasiness about the street work, and it has been helpful for our staffers to discuss their problems openly because they find that there are others who are struggling through the same situation.

One night after we had conducted a street meeting, we had no sooner walked into our apartment than Cindy began crying. There seemed to be no explanation for the sudden flood of tears, but when she was able to speak Cindy told me, "Tonight

Dave asked me in front of the whole group how many souls I had led to Christ. I was so embarrassed."

I took her hand in mine. It didn't do any good; she began crying all over again.

"Honey," I said, "Dave wasn't trying to embarrass you. He just wanted to find out how you were doing."

Cindy wiped the tears from her eyes and began again: "I try to talk to people, but I can't seem to get through to them.

I explained to her that this was a difficult type of work, that trying to gain the attention of juvenile delinquents was far from easy. "All you need is some more experience working among these people," I told her. "Once you find the knack of communicating with these youngsters you'll be all right."

A few days later a group of college students who had come to work with us during the summer went with us to a small park near a cluster of apartment houses in Brooklyn. As usual, the first ones to gather around us as we began our evening's ministry were some children who were attracted by music we played. After a few more minutes, a handful of teenagers came over and a group of girls seated on the nearby benches stopped their chattering so they could hear what we had to say. Once we had gotten their attention—the first step in this type of street ministry—we began handing out tracts concerning our work at Teen Challenge. Things went according to the general pattern, with the boys exhibiting interest and curiosity about our work and the girls turning up their noses at the mention of religion. During a lull in the activity, I glanced around to see if I could spot Cindy. To my surprise I saw her witnessing nonstop to the girls who were seated on the benches.

Several years ago I gained new appreciation of how vastly different our street-corner ministry is from the methods used by most Christians. It all began when a dedicated gentleman came to visit Teen Challenge. He was the author of a number of books about how easy personal evangelism was; he and many of his readers as well had proved that the job of leading men to salvation through Christ was not as difficult as some people believe. Their successes came as the result of using a systematic approach in dealing with the needs of people.

I remember well the enthusiasm with which he spoke about

this method of his; I shared with him the joy of his accomplishments. And I also remember his eagerness as he awaited the opportunity to put his system into practice on the street corners of Brooklyn. I am certain that he fully expected to be able to step out onto those street corners and win youngsters over by the droves. Well, the time came for us to venture out onto those streets and he joined with us.

By the time the evening's work was over and we had returned to the Center, he had found that trying to use a carefully outlined approach in dealing with these youngsters was useless. He learned that these were a breed far different from those he had encountered in other parts of the country. Trying to get through to them according to a set formula was about as impossible as trying to shovel out a snowed-in driveway with a teaspoon. I can still hear him saying that night, "I think I'll leave this work to you fellows. I'm going back home to use my outline. It works there."

None of us thought any the less of him. We knew what he was going through, having all experienced similar setbacks and days of deep discouragement.

Hundreds of times I have been asked the question, "How many professionals do you have on your staff at Teen Challenge?" In the terms these questioners are thinking of, we have no professionals. They are talking about psychiatrists, medical doctors, social workers and other highly educated individuals. I always make a point of telling these people that, although none of our staffers is accredited in these fields, they are all professionals—professional Christians trying to be of service to mankind. Our workers are consecrated men and women, and those of them who have become ordained ministers have had to learn to suppress their own desires to stand in a pulpit and deliver eloquent sermons. We have all found that the best sermons we have preached have been those addressed to one needy person who was willing to listen. Our task is to find a way to deal with the individual who is in need, each one so different from the next. When you work with him on a person-to-person basis you cannot waste a word, for unless his needs are met at that moment it may be too late.

Most of our work during the early years was among gang

members. How weak they were! How young they were! It was their youth, perhaps more than anything else, that made me want to weep. These were not like the teenagers I had grown up with in Pennsylvania. I had never thought that such young people existed. Even when I had heard about youngsters such as these there had never entered my mind any pictures of the terrible conditions in which they lived. Never having been exposed to them, there had been no way for me to comprehend their kind of existence. Now that I was working with these teenagers at point-blank range, I could better understand a few things. Now I could see why Dave had not let me become more involved in the work during my first term of service with him; and I could also see why he had wanted me to mature a little before I plunged into this endeavor.

The pastor of one of the local churches told us that we could use his church as a meeting place for groups of young boys and girls. Getting kids off those streets and into a church was an answer to prayer. It was not, however, the answer to all our problems in trying to reach these young people. One of the chief concerns was trying to keep our listeners alert once we had convinced them to come to church and had actually gotten them there. Addicts who came generally tended to be groggy, either because they had recently shot up with drugs or because they were just plain weary. Gang members who were not drug addicts were usually under the influence of cheap wine or whiskey. I'd look out over an audience of nodding heads and I'd wistfully recall my little church in Barre, Vermont.

Once in a while some of the youngsters would heckle us in church, but others would invariably quiet them by saying, "Come on, man, these cats are tryin' to help us." Most of them didn't want our help; yet they respected us for what we were trying to accomplish. Underneath their façade of toughness there was, I am certain, a fear of God that made them tolerate us. One thing I know: you don't find atheists among these young people.

There were several instances when they showed their respect in rather unique ways. One of the gang leaders would sidle up to us before a service and say, "Look, we promised we'd be here, but—uh—well, we're gonna have to leave at 8:15. We got a rumble at 8:30." We were powerless to stop gang fights, so we tried to live as best we could in the midst of them. Sometimes it was hard. It wasn't too difficult when you knew that the boys were going to be leaving at 8:30. But sometimes you'd be in the middle of a well-planned message you were delivering to them and a gang member would burst into the church and shout, "There's a rumble. Let's go." Before your eyes, you would see a congregation arise with a oneness when they heard their comrade's distress call. It was frustrating, yet I had to admire the eloquence of anyone who, with so few words, had been able to arouse an entire congregation.

There was one night when we were in the Brownsville section of Brooklyn, which is a few miles north of the Center, and we were told that we should forget about having a meeting. One of the boys warned us that a small rumble was soon to take place. Instead of going back to the Center, though, we stayed right where we were, in a small apartment that we had rented for use as a chapel. While we sat in the chapel we were able to see the rumble as it raged in the streets. We had seen others, and we were to see more in the future; and it had been our experience that one of the best times to deal with gang members was right after a battle. Many were in particular need of spiritual advice at times like that. Some were grieving because a comrade had been injured. Others were penitent because they had hurt someone else. When the flush of excitement had worn off after the rumble, many of these combatants saw things more realistically than they had before and they could see that what they were up to was wrong.

Boys like Legs and Sundown and Chino would sit in the chapel after a melee. Half an hour before they had been screaming, intent upon mayhem. Now they were silent. The wounded wiped away the blood. At times such as this these teenagers were more receptive to what we had to say than on many other days when our planning had been much more elaborate.

It was a work filled with setbacks. No sooner would we seem to be establishing a firm contact with a boy than we would get word that he had been picked up by the police. Or we would find out that he had been injured in a street fight and wouldn't be out of the hospital for several months—if at all. Life in Brownsville was like that in most of Brooklyn— filled with violence that could strike anyone at any time in any place. Two of our workers were having a talk with a boy named Eddie in front of our chapel in Brownsville one summer evening. While they were talking, another boy came up and plunged a knife into Eddie's midsection. Eddie was rushed to the hospital and, thanks to modern surgical methods and his own recuperative powers, was back on the streets in four or five months. But he would never again be able to roam the streets with a peaceful mind. Neither would the thousands of others who were beaten up, shot, stabbed, and abused on the sidewalks of Brooklyn.

Still, I found my heart going out to these people. When I had first come to work among them they had frightened me and I hadn't understood them or their way of life. Now I was beginning to comprehend, to see the sociological upheaval that was spewing these people into the streets and sidewalks and gutters. Hundreds of thousands of people shoehorned into this tiny corner of earth, many of them poorly educated, many of them jobless, many of them bewildered by the world that pressed in on them from all sides.

Hope? Fun? Goals? Incentives? Family life? These people knew none of these things. They existed, rather than lived, which was tragic in itself, but what made it even worse was that they had a hard time finding a reason for existing. And the street—the street was the neighborhood living room. Parties were held in the street. Bottles and cans were thrown by those at the party proper, as well as by those on the fifth floor who leaned out the window, drank a toast and then flung away their empties. Fights were held in the street. Buying and selling were done in the street. Loves were won and lost in the street. So were lives. Often there was more concern over a lost love than over a lost life. Streets were where parents sent their kids when they wanted privacy. It was in those streets that kids seemed to age a year each month, their hearts growing colder and colder during those days when they should have known the warmth of home.

Fighting—a way of life

They were caught up in a gang life that swept away freedom, individuality, and hope—the very things they were so frantically searching for. That was one of the unwritten laws of gang life: the gang giveth *and* the gang taketh away. It took gang members little time to become beholden to the gang and its leaders. When an order was given to them by a superior, they soon learned to obey—with Marine-like swiftness—or else. Never will I forget the expression of hopelessness on the face of one boy with whom I was talking about his plight; he admitted that he was wrong and then added, "But you don't understand that we *gotta* fight."

And fight they did. They fought to protect their nationality, the color of their skin, the honor of the parents they hardly knew, the dignity of a gang that was founded for the purposes of circumventing the law. Then, too, there was always another of the most noble of all warfares in Brooklyn: the rumble to preserve the majesty, tradition and reputation of The Block.

It was a society filled with incongruities. Boys too young to shave were carrying eight-inch stilettoes. Youngsters unable to get a passing grade in even the simplest tests in school were capable of masterminding gangs of fifty or more.

It was the sort of work that sent me to bed totally exhausted, yet which all too often left me wide awake as I stared into the darkness. These were real-life people and if their problems were not solved, more than a few of them would soon not be real—or live.

Helping to rebuild the lives of youngsters such as this gave me a new confidence. No sooner was I beginning to feel at ease in my work, though, than two situations arose to unsettle me. One was Dave's numerous trips away from New York, trips that threw an increasing workload on me. The other was the sudden, swift and ominous rise of drug addiction in New York. Whether Dave was gone for a day or two or for a week's crusade, I could hardly wait for his return so that I could be relieved of the decision-making and other tasks that I had inherited during his absence. Unfortunately, the problem of drug addiction did not come and go as did Dave; it had arrived and it was obvious that it was going to remain.

One of my earliest encounters with the situation came on

a day when I was looking for a boy named Chino, a muscular youngster with bulging biceps and sturdy shoulders. I wandered over to the area or turf where his gang hung out and when I didn't see Chino I began asking the other boys where he was.

"You lookin' for Chino?" one boy asked me. "You won't find him here. Don't you know, he's not a jitterbugger [gang fighter] any more. He's on the needle. Go over to the park and look for the junkies. You'll find Chino over there with them."

When I got to the park, sure enough, I saw Chino. At first I didn't think it was Chino—his shoulders were slumped, his cheeks were hollow and his arms looked skinny.

"What happened to you, Chino?" I asked.

"Man, jitterbuggin' is for kids. Dope's the kick now."

Chino had traded in his knife for a needle. Thousands of other Chinos were making the same trade.

four /...
... / "here I am, such as
/ there is left of me"

A FEW SHORT YEARS ago the problems of coping with gangs seemed insurmountable. Gangs were so strong, so large, so numerous and so well organized that the police could not handle them. When drugs became readily accessible to anyone who wanted them, the gang members made full use of them. In doing so, they became more individualistic—less interested in and dependent upon the gang and more concerned with their own need for dope. Thus, instead of sharing the loot from their robberies with their fellow gang members, they kept the money so they could buy drugs. As these men and boys drifted off singly or in pairs and began to look out only for themselves, the structure of the gangs soon began to crumble.

Gangs, once so powerful that the law could not even come close to breaking them up, were wiped out by drugs. If that seems to indicate that drugs are, as such, stronger than the law, it is true. Spurred on by addicts who need large amounts of money to buy their drugs, the crime rate in the New York area has become frightening. Drug usage has become so widespread and commonplace that it has reached almost catastrophic proportions and threatens our very society and nation, not just New York.

Our work was not limited to addicts and gangs. We extended our outreach to help prostitutes, alcoholics, and people with a wide range of other problems. People frequently thrust themselves upon us, begging for help. Parents came with children who had resisted the counseling of highly trained doctors or penal authorities. Judging by the standards of the world, we knew that we were not qualified to cope with such a diverse number of cases.

The only thing that kept us going—and this is as true today as it was then—was that we prayed about our needs and could feel God's leading in these matters. Had we proceeded on our own, we would surely have done irrevocable harm and probably would have brought Teen Challenge tumbling down around us. With God answering our prayers and interceding for us in so many ways, though, we moved forward.

Just as our work was not limited to one or two types of people, so it was not limited to the Brooklyn area. We branched out all across New York City. Often we deliberately sought out the worst places to do our work, spots like 122nd Street and Lexington Avenue in Manhattan or along Fox Street in The Bronx, one of the most notorious locations in the world of drugs. How bad was Fox Street? Probably no better description has been given than that offered by one of our workers when he said that "the only decent people on the block are the alcoholics."

Our workers consisted largely of students from Bible colleges who volunteered to work with us. When we sent workers into some of these more chaotic neighborhoods we made certain that we sent them in clusters of ten or more. We have been cautioned and criticized again and again by the police, by ministers and by friends for permitting our staffers—especially the girls—to be out on those streets late at night and often early into the next morning. We have persisted in this method because we have found this to be the best way to reach the needy.

One of the most significant phases of our street ministry is the open-air meetings in which groups of our workers present the message of Christ in song and testimony. For downright effectiveness we have found it impossible to beat a testimony given by a converted drug addict on a street corner to a gathering of people who are presently addicted. There is a certain empathy there between speaker and hearer that cannot be duplicated.

When one of these converts steps up to the microphone to give his or her testimony we can usually notice an increase

Open-air meeting conducted by former addict
on street where he lived

Teen Challenge worker talks to addicts "on the nod" (under influence of heroin). *Below:* A "tea party." Smoking marijuana nearly always leads to desire for higher "highs," heroin or LSD, for instance.

in the interest level among our listeners. People nudge each other and say, "Hey, that really is Poncho." Conversations among knots of people suddenly break up and they all turn to listen. Many who would not listen to a minister preach a sermon are now avidly listening because the speaker is someone they know, someone they have shared a portion of their life with, someone who, just as they had done, had despaired and decided that life was no longer worth living. Youngsters can invariably be seen scurrying down the block calling out, "Hey, guess who's on the corner of 112th Street. It's Poncho. He's got religion and now he's off drugs." These are the youngsters who had heard about drugs, had watched people become slaves to it—perhaps a brother, an uncle, a father or mother. Seeing someone like Poncho was to them like seeing someone returned from the dead.

Few converts have had as effective a testimony as Cookie Rivera. She grew up on Fox Street and everyone there knew her. When Cookie got up during our street meetings and gave her testimony, it was hard for these people to believe this was the same girl.

"Look at me," Cookie would say. "This is Cookie. You remember me; we shot drugs together. Jose," she said to a tall Puerto Rican, "you remember the night we took off together." Jose would nod his head. "Well, this is a different Cookie now. No more stuff. No more prostituting. No more working angles. God changed my life. You can see what He's done to me. I'm here to tell you that Jesus is real and that He can heal the dope addict."

One of the hardest things for addicts to comprehend is that they *can* be helped. There is perhaps no more difficult barrier for us to break through in reaching these people than a wicked motto with which they have been brainwashed: "Once an addict, always an addict." They have heard these words so often that they are convinced that there is no cure for them—until a Poncho or a Cookie shows up. This is the way Cookie tells her story, and it may give you an appreciation of why many of those who remember what she was like when they were growing up together find it hard to believe that she is now living a pure life.

"I was born in Puerto Rico into a home where my mother herself was a baby—fourteen and a half years old. My father had committed suicide before my birth. My mother remarried and my father's mother became my new mother. My goal in life was to be a high school teacher so that my grandmother would not have to work any more. Friends told me I could get the necessary education in New York City, so we sold all our possessions and took an airplane to New York City.

"Our arrival in the middle of New York City at 42nd Street was a shock—men dressed like women, women dressed like men, young people smoking and drinking in the streets.

"I could not speak English. How could we look for an apartment if I didn't know how to converse in English or get around the city? Also, there was discrimination against Spanish-speaking people. The only choice left was to live with my uncle, his wife, three children, an aunt, and a cousin. Nine of us in one small furnished room. We lived like this for a year; then got a place of our own in Harlem.

"Our new apartment was a palace to us. It had five rooms, but the neighborhood was a jungle. It was wild. We stayed in Harlem for a year. Soon I realized I was not the same girl who had stepped off that airplane from Puerto Rico. It was necessary for me to belong to a gang to be safe in the streets. Anyway, I wanted to belong. It all started with the small vices —smoking and drinking. Then I became rebellious. I hated any kind of authority: police, parental, or school. I played hooky from school, got drunk every night. But my heart was empty.

"Something bigger came along—marijuana. I took my first puff on a marijuana cigarette when I was fourteen. It was the beginning of a mental habit. I wouldn't go to school unless I was high on pot. Then heroin became my god.

"About a year after I started using heroin, I thought if I fell in love that I would be able to stop using drugs. Having a baby didn't change me, however. It only created more problems. I tried hospitals. A woman psychiatrist told me the only way I would change would be to go back to Puerto Rico. Back in Puerto Rico it was all the same. No way out. I returned to the city.

"One morning at five o'clock a former drug addict came to

me and started talking to me about Jesus. I laughed at him. Instead of slapping my face as I deserved, he put his head down and started crying. He told me that Jesus loved me and wanted to use my life. I looked at him and said, 'If this Jesus Christ could use me and could change my life, then I would like to give Him a try.' He gave me the address of Teen Challenge.

"It was on a Friday night that I entered the Center. Three weeks went by and during this time I saw addicts transformed. I couldn't believe this was possible, for I was very hard. I just couldn't accept Christ and give my life over to Him.

"Dave Wilkerson was invited to preach in Pittsburgh and I was asked to go. The Teen Challenge staff prayed that God would break me that night. Since I had returned from Puerto Rico, I had never cried, even though people hurt me. In other words, I had a rock for a heart. When the altar call was given, I decided that Christ was the only answer. I put my hands up, closed my eyes, and asked Christ to make Himself real to me, to make me cry, and to break me completely. My real problem was hatred and sin, not drug addiction.

"At that moment, I experienced something more than fighting, smoking marijuana, drinking, or heroin had to offer, and that was love, peace, and joy. In front of everyone, I cried. The tears were real. Only Christ could soften my stony heart by breaking it and taking possession."

Occasionally, people at our street meetings tearfully tell us their stories and ask us to take them to the Center with us right away. This we do, if we have room and if we feel that they are sincere. In the case of drug addicts, though, we often put them to a test first, one that is designed to find out if they mean business. We have found that too many addicts want to come to the Center for nothing more than a good meal, a chance to wash up, and for a bed to sleep in. That kind can have a demoralizing effect on others in our program who have been trying their hardest to resist the temptations around them. What we want is desperate men and women—the kind who may be afraid of the pain of withdrawing from drugs but who are not afraid to suffer if they can find a newness of life. To the addict, therefore, we like to say, "You're welcome to come to the Center—tomorrow morning." Then, if they have been able to fight off the craving for drugs and make the trip to the Center the next morning, we gladly take them in.

On my way into the Center one morning I saw a young man slumped on the front steps. As he lifted his head I could see the tell-tale signs of pain and sorrow in his eyes and face. Then I saw a small smile creep across his lips.

"You told me to come back this morning," he said. "Yesterday when you interviewed me you told me to come back in the morning. Rode the subways most of the night. Had to keep changing trains so the cops wouldn't pick me up. I made it. Here I am, such as there is left of me."

When he had uttered those last words—"Here I am, such as there is left of me"—I wanted to clutch him to my breast and weep tears of hope and joy. It was too early, however, to become that aroused, for as I opened the door and let this man into the Center I knew that there were long and painful days between him and a cure.

When we ask someone to come the following day we stress that we don't want him to put off his arrival any longer than that. I know of a drug addict who was going to come to Teen Challenge and kept telling himself that "tomorrow" would be his day to come to the Center. As it turned out, it took him three years to make the 15-minute trip; on one of those days of his indecision the police picked him up and he was sentenced to three years in prison.

For those of us who have never used drugs, it is impossible to know how powerful a grip they can take on the mind and body. But we do know that drug addiction, like all habits, is hard to overcome. What makes it so difficult for an addict is that drugs act as a destructive agent on his will power. Without the will power to clean himself of drugs, an addict has no hope. A mere desire to end his addiction is never sufficient. That's why I explain to them that the only way they can be cured is through a new kind of will power—their will and God's power.

One of the benefits of our years of labor is that we are now recognized and accepted in many neighborhoods. It is always a thrill to be walking down a street and hear some youngster say, "Hi, Reverend." And it has been even more comforting on those occasions when someone is giving me a hard time and one of his friends comes along and tells him, "Cool it, man. He's okay. He's with Teen Challenge." Having a rapport like this has enabled us to walk where even the police fear to tread.

The name Teen Challenge has become known by the people of the night. They seem to appreciate our attempts to help them and they all admit they need aid. Sometimes they come up to us just to talk about the weather or sports or to say a few aimless words, as though they derive a comfort from being able to make small talk with someone who is not trying to exploit some angle or pressure them in some way.

We had to overcome many obstacles in order to attain our present status among New Yorkers. It has not been easy to gain the confidence of drug addicts and criminals, who are always glancing over their shoulders, wary that they might be stopped at any moment by a plainclothes policeman or narcotics agent. On top of that, we have also had to gain the confidence of the police. There was one night when a group of us had made a trip to a neighborhood that was saturated with drugs. Addicts were scurrying around trying to locate pushers so they could buy some drugs. Others, who had already shot up with drugs, were nodding on the street corners, some of them leaning against lamp posts to keep from falling down. Then along came several policemen and guess who they ordered off the streets? That's right, they told *us* to get on our way.

But that was back in our early days, back when we were having such a hard time establishing ourselves and making ourselves and our purpose understood. Still, we are forever being asked by members of the police force, "What are you people doing in a place like this?" Whenever a group goes out to do some street work, we can always rely on at least one or two policemen asking us such questions. Although we have never done it, we have often kidded that we should hire one person whose sole responsibility it would be to answer the questions of these policemen.

Because I have had numerous opportunities to speak with the members of New York's police force, I have come to appreciate their concern for us. I have also come to sympathize with the policemen, who so often see the dirtiest and most underprivileged neighborhoods. Day after day they must cope with drug addicts and delinquents and life in the ghettos. It is easy to understand why some of them become bitter. One policeman told me, "The only way to handle these drug addicts is to take them over to the Brooklyn Bridge and shove them off one by one."

One day, one of our workers was driving a busload of boys back to the Center when a policeman ordered him to pull over and asked who he was and where he was going.

"I'm from Teen Challenge and I'm bringing these fellows back from church," he told the policeman.

"Oh, sure you are," said the policeman with a smile that would have chilled a polar bear. "Now why don't you just come along with me and tell that one to the sergeant down at headquarters."

Later that evening I got a call from the boy at the police headquarters. I managed to speak to the police officer in charge and explained that the young man was, indeed, a member of our staff and that we were working among the gangs and that we were not ourselves a gang.

Winning the confidence of the police and the people has been a major accomplishment which has made our task much easier. During the first few years of trying to prove ourselves, we knew that everyone with whom we came in contact was scrutinizing us. They sought to find chinks in our armor: Were we really a self-seeking group that had some ulterior motive? Were we a hypocritical lot of people, a bunch of do-gooders? Did we have any knowledge of how to help those we were seeking to lend a hand to? What went on behind the doors at Teen Challenge?

We could tell these people anything we wanted to, could preach to them at length and could offer them assistance, but we soon discovered that unless we could show them some results it would be all in vain. Addicts had so often been offered cures and so often they had been disappointed.

Then, one by one, addicts stepped out of Teen Challenge, returned to their neighborhoods and became living testimonies for the curative powers of Christ. There are always a few in every neighborhood who are undergoing some cure to try to kick their habit; the other addicts watch them with interest. Then, as those who are seeking to be rescued from drugs fail in their attempts, they fall back into the bottomless pit and all the addicts seem to say in unison, "Once an addict, always an addict." We have heard of hundreds of cases of addicts who have kicked the habit for days, weeks and even months. They felt they were clean, that they had gained the victory. Invariably, they succumbed to temptation and fell victim to a worse addiction to narcotics than before.

Addicts went to hospitals and willingly went through periods of withdrawal, therapy and rehabilitation. Confident, they returned to their environment and were quickly swallowed up. Others underwent psychiatric care, voluntary withdrawal or tried an assortment of pills to try to rid themselves of their need for narcotics. Their will power enabled some of them to gain a temporary freedom from drugs, but before long they were back on heroin. It was no wonder that they lived in despair. Thus it was that addicts frowned upon anyone and everyone who offered a cure. They knew better—they felt that it was better to have no hope at all than to have a false hope.

But when addicts left Teen Challenge, able to demonstrate that their lives had been transformed and that they could live without drugs, the junkies took an interest. Their curiosity was aroused. What were we doing and what did we have that no one else had? We explained to them that the key to our success was not man-made—that the cornerstone of our program was Christ. In times past we were often sneered at when we tried to get this point across, but now that reformed addicts were becoming living proof for us, other addicts were willing to listen. We told them we had found that it was almost impossible for men to overcome drugs only on the strength of their will power or with pills and that the best way was to rely on the strength of Christ. It was not easy for these people to comprehend what we were talking about; yet they were intrigued and were willing to admit that they needed a strength more dependable than their own.

Slowly, one painstaking step at a time, Teen Challenge was

emerging as a vital force; the addicts, the delinquents, and the lost all understood that they could trust us and that the help we were offering them was not just another myth. The police believed in our sincerity. And Teen Challenge was returning to society a group of people who had been revitalized and who now had something to live for.

five /...
... / 416

"THERE'S A WHOLE CITY out there waiting for you," Dave said to me one evening. "Thousands of people are in need and if we're going to help them we have to bring these people in. What we need more than anything is someone who can direct all of our evangelistic efforts and also live right in the Center so he can be on top of all that goes on. I think you're the man for the job, Don. The opportunity is waiting for you. Are you willing to accept?"

"I don't know what to say," was the best reply I could come up with on the spot.

"There's a whole city out there waiting for you," Dave repeated.

As much as I knew that Dave liked prompt answers, I had to tell him that this was something I would have to mull over and then discuss with Cindy. Deep down, I knew that I wanted to accept Dave's offer. What I wasn't sure about was whether I wanted to get as involved with the work as Dave was. In the back of my mind there still flickered a hope that I might be the pastor of a rural church, an ambition that I might have to forsake for good if I accepted Dave's offer.

Once I had made up my mind I would be willing to move to the Center and coordinate all of our evangelistic work, I prepared for the second phase of this policy-making decision. This was a verdict in which Cindy would have to share, but, knowing how much she disliked city life, I was dubious about her agreeing to move to the Center in Brooklyn. So I attempted to make the whole thing sound like a once-in-a-lifetime-dream-come-true, putting on my best smile and cheeriest voice as I asked her, "Honey, how would you like to live right in the Center?"

Instead of giving me a list of reasons why we should not move to the Center, Cindy said she liked the idea. The more she talked about it, the more she liked it. What convinced her to make the move, I think, was that for the first time in nearly a year and a half we could leave Staten Island and have an apartment of our own at 416. We had no idea of what we were letting ourselves in for, however. Living at the Center meant that there was no escape from the work at Teen Challenge. Now we lived with Teen Challenge. Its sounds and its problems—as well as those of the neighborhood—were with us constantly.

Teen Challenge was undergoing many changes. One of the most significant was that we were housing more needy cases in 416. No longer were we just dealing with people on the streets and bringing a few of them to the Center. As long as that had been the situation, almost all those people we dealt with on the streets or in services at the Center had gone home at night and had taken their problems with them. Now that we were able to bring more of them into the Center to live, they were becoming a part of our family and their heartaches became our heartaches.

Addicts, for the most part, were graduates of gang life and were old enough to stay with us without need for parental consent. Unlike those people we had been working with, addicts needed closer supervision. These men and women were harder to control; supervision of them became a 24-hour-a-day job. No longer was I able to wrap up my street ministry and feel that my day's work was over. Now there were problems of being in charge of all our evangelistic efforts, of taking care of increasing stacks of paper work, and of being just as ready to respond to a crisis at 4 in the morning as to one at 4 in the afternoon. It wasn't long before I felt the pressure of this new job.

The work was rewarding, nevertheless. There were always converts around the Center, people who had been rehabilitated and were now free of drugs. They were an encouragement to all of us. After having been with us for several weeks, one

Out of the depths . . . new hope.

Above: Ghetto playground. *Right:* 416 Clinton Avenue, Teen Challenge induction center.

addict said, "As soon as I walked through the door I knew that this place was different from all the rest." That was a high compliment, for this man had been on drugs for years. When he referred to "all the rest," he meant the other places he had gone to try to kick his habit—federal and state hospitals, mental institutions and numerous clinics. Watching men such as this rid themselves of drugs and begin to live useful lives made all the hours of labor worthwhile.

To make it sound all that simple would not be honest, though. It didn't take long to learn that we couldn't take in anyone and everyone. Some of these people weren't serious about seeking our aid. They took advantage of us in many ways; each time that one of them stole from us or walked out on us the unrest they caused among other addicts at the Center set our program back another notch. It soon became evident that our process of selecting and admitting people would have to be refined. This was not easily worked out, for judging the sincerity of addicts, we were finding out, was a delicate matter. One of our earliest strategies, telling an addict who sought admittance that he should come back the next day, was a method that we found to be one of the most reliable tests of how much he yearned to get rid of his habit. Rarely have I made an exception to this rule. I recall one day when a female addict was in my office pleading for help.

"You can't let me go back out to the streets," she said. "I came all the way from The Bronx because I heard that you want to help addicts."

"You're high on drugs," I told her. "I can't let you in here in your condition."

"I'm not high." Then, realizing that I knew better, she added, "Well, maybe a little. Please, you gotta let me stay."

I could see that she needed help and yet I knew that anyone in her state could not make a rational decision. People like her would promise themselves one day that they would do anything to get clean of drugs but when the drugs wore off they would not be able to curb their craving for more heroin.

"Come back tomorrow," I told her.

"Listen, mister, I need help *now*."

I knew that two men were waiting outside for the girl and

by this time I was familiar enough with the dope racket to realize what their function was. They were the ones who sold her talents as a prostitute, taking the money to buy drugs so that all three could shoot up with heroin.

"I'm sorry," I said. "I just can't let you in." The words were hard to utter, but I felt I had to be firm.

"Mister, I·want help. Please, please, please."

Reluctantly, I gave in to her request. I have never regretted it, for this was Cookie Rivera. She has remained free of drugs for years, has become a staunch Christian, a fine wife and mother, and has helped many others to cleanse their lives.

Another time I broke my own rule was when I asked a young man why he had come to Teen Challenge and he replied, "Ah, my old lady wanted me to come." I let him stay because I appreciated his honesty. Fortunately, he fulfilled my hopes for him and kicked his dope habit.

An eye-opener that gave me an insight into an angle I had to be aware of in the future was Benny's case. After being with us for a short time, Benny walked out. When he came back he was penitent. I told him that he could rejoin our program but warned him, "Don't leave again, because there may not be a next time." Well, Benny took off again for a few hours and when he came back he asked to be readmitted. "I think the Lord is talking to me," he said. "I think He wants me to stay here this time." Again, I broke my rule about readmitting anyone, this time warning Benny that this would positively be his final chance.

Benny soon underwent a remarkable transformation. During his earlier stays he had been one of the most disruptive men we had ever had in our program, arguing with counselors and mocking the word of God. Now, though, he became a different person. He accepted Christ one night, and after that he became a model patient. After a few weeks of exemplary behavior, however, Benny confessed that the real reason for his having returned to us twice was because he was a parole viola-tor and that he was using Teen Challenge merely as a place to hide from the police.

"I never thought I'd be telling you this," Benny said, "but now that I have Christ in my heart I know that what I am doing is wrong. I'd like to turn myself over to the police so I won't have to keep on running from them."

Benny's story is a complicated one, but he has persevered through extremely difficult days and is now studying for the ministry.

These have all been examples of times I have violated my own rules and have not had to regret such decisions. Sad to say, my intuition has not always been so accurate.

When someone enters our program, I tell him, "You are coming into a different world. You are coming out of a deep, deep darkness and the light will be hard to get used to. There will be some things that we do here that you won't agree with or understand. All we ask is that you keep your heart and mind open to God and let Him show you the way to a new life."

If the person is a drug addict, as most of them are at this time, we explain that our program is not an easy one and that he will have to shake his drug habit without the help of any medication. This is called "cold turkey." It is an agonizing ordeal. Those who go through with it suffer severe withdrawal pains that immobilize them, sending them through two, three or four days of sweaty torment and delirium. They also come down with cold shivers, leg cramps, stomach cramps, vomiting and dizziness. Sleep comes only fitfully and is marked by nightmares and, occasionally, by screaming. It is impossible not to suffer with these people. Just learning how to become involved in their plight in a Christian way was something that had to be worked at and prayed about.

Almost all medical experts scorned the use of cold turkey back at the time when we were first beginning to work with addicts. Our method, though, is slightly different from that which the experts are used to. Our form of cold turkey comes complete with one added ingredient which we apply in liberal doses: Christian love for our fellow men.

Just how valuable this added ingredient is can be seen in the words of one addict who underwent cold turkey both without it and then with it. "Once when I had to kick the habit in jail, I vomited, I had diarrhea, and I shook all over," he says. "For three or four days I couldn't sleep and I couldn't eat. When I kicked at Teen Challenge, I ached some, but after two days I was eating three meals a day. How can you feel sick where everyone's always looking out for you and trying to help and asking, 'How do you feel? Can I rub your back or get you some food?' "

During these first days and nights we keep constant watch over them and try to comfort them in every way possible. Our staffers and other former addicts who are part of our program spend hours sitting at the bedside of a person going through withdrawal. Sometimes addicts want you to sit at their bedside and talk to them, or to wipe the sweat from their faces, or to read to them from the Bible. Someone always brings a tray of food to them at mealtimes, hoping that these new men will take a little nourishment. Usually, though, it is several days before they feel like eating. Counselors visit with them and pray for them and assure them that the Lord will provide them with all the strength they will need. It is all part of our efforts to let these new ones know that we care about them. More than anything, it is a little bit of love that we are showing, a commodity that has been so scarce in their lives.

Why do we subject a drug addict to cold turkey? This is not something that we want to do. It is done because we have found it absolutely essential. We have to find out as soon as possible if a person is desperate for help. It has been our experience that unless someone is desperate, unless he has exhausted all other hope and unless he has reached the brink of despair, he rarely can be helped. That is why we deliberately knock all the props out from under him, hoping that when he is able to stand up he will reach out and rely completely on the strength of God to carry him from there.

When an addict has made it through cold turkey he is given a list of rules he must obey:

TEEN CHALLENGE HOUSE RULES

1. Absolutely NO SMOKING!
2. No talking about the street life or drugs. No cursing.
3. No conversations with staff members of the opposite sex.
4. No one will be permitted to leave the Center during the first seven weeks except in an extreme emergency. In case of emergency, you will not be able to go alone.

5. Upon entering Teen Challenge, you must know that you are to seek the Lord. If you have any family problems, health problems, teeth problems, or court problems you must take care of them all before entering our program.

6. All permissions are given by the staff member in charge.

7. Everyone must attend chapel, prayer time, and classes, with Bibles (unless kicking).

8. Haircuts will be given any time that it is convenient for the staff.

9. All are required to attend the Y.M.C.A. program.

10. No guest is allowed in the rooms.

11. No one will be permitted to have more than one dollar at a time.

12. All visits are on Saturday and Sunday only. No outside visits or permission will be given during the week. (No visits during first week.)

13. Everyone is required to do a regular duty, plus extra duties during work periods, and all duties must be done before going out.

14. All phone calls must be handled on the pay phone. No phone calls are allowed during chapel, class, or prayer time.

15. We request that all rooms be neat and clean before anyone is allowed to eat.

16. No one is allowed an overnight visit before going to the farm.

17. Lights are to be out at 11:30 P.M. weekdays and 12:00 P.M. on weekends.

18. Anyone who needs extra money for cleaning, haircuts, etc. will be allowed extra work with approval of Dean or Assistant.

19. No one is allowed in kitchen except those working there.

20. All staff members are here for one reason—to help you find the Lord. They are not too busy for your problems.

I made a point of talking over the rules with everyone in our program, emphasizing Rule 4 more than any other. "There are no bars on the windows here, no cells in which we will keep you locked up," I would tell them. "The front door is never locked. You can walk out any time you feel like it. But if you do, you're through. We won't let you back in."

One of the most common reactions after an addict reads the rules is, "This place is like a jail." Another frequently heard comment is, "Nobody trusts you around here."

"You are absolutely right," I tell such complainers. "Nobody around here is going to trust you. You're still a dope addict. You haven't kicked your habit yet. As soon as we see evidence that you want to change and are making some progress, then we'll begin to trust you. But you'll have to earn your trust."

"Reverend," some of them will say to me, "you've never been on drugs, have you?"

By now I know the routine. As soon as I say, "No, I've never used drugs," they pounce on me by saying, "Then you just don't understand how I feel. How can you be any help to an addict if you've never been one?" Whereupon I reply, "Does a doctor have to have cancer to treat someone who has the disease? Does he have to have a broken leg to help a person who has one?" That usually takes care of that situation.

Once an addict has gone through cold turkey we do everything possible to assist him. The first thing we must often do is provide these people with clothing. For this we take them to what we call our Blessing Room, a room where we keep clothes that have been donated to us. Clothing is much more vital to the rehabilitation of an addict than we thought at first. They have great concern about what they wear and a strong desire to be neat. Patched shirts or trousers or scuffed shoes are usually refused or only reluctantly accepted. These new entrants feel that the offer of shabby clothing is a sign of our contempt. Although they realize they cannot be too choosy, they have let us know in no unmistakable terms that they want to look respectable. We do our best to clothe them neatly, knowing that an addict who feels that he is being treated like a second-class citizen is quick to harbor resentment. Such an attitude, we have learned through painful experience, can be the initial step in leading a person away from Teen Challenge.

Some addicts have nothing to wear except the rags they come in with. Others, however, have stashed their clothes in various cleaning establishments around the city. The reason for this is that many of them who have no real home where they could keep clothes have felt that the safest thing for them to do was to leave a shirt at one cleaner, a pair of trousers at another cleaner and so on. When they remember that they have left their clothing in half a dozen places we help them get it back piece by piece. We drive them around to the various cleaners and also let them do extra work around the Center—for which they earn 50 to 75 cents an hour—so that they can pay for their clothing. Most of them receive clothes from their loved ones once their progress in overcoming their addiction to drugs becomes evident.

Love, clothing, and food all help the narcotics user to kick his habit, gain a measure of self-respect and a feeling that there is a purpose to life that heretofore has escaped him. This purpose is centered on Jesus Christ, who has turned darkness into light for millions of men during the past 2,000 years. When a drug addict—or any man, woman or child, for that matter—decides that he has a desire to live, he must next find what he wants to live for, what he wants to focus his life upon. Countless numbers of people have built their lives around a quest for money, but history has proved that the rich die no happier than the poor. Other people have centered their lives on such things as their families, their jobs, their hobbies, their homes. Ultimately, though, all men die, and it is only those who have met with Christ Jesus and accepted Him into their hearts who have a true glimpse of the fact that there is yet a much more rewarding life to be lived by those who have believed on Him.

Because Christ is our strength for the present and our hope for the future, we make every effort to help sincere men and women in our program accept Him as their Savior. Those who welcome Jesus into their lives find that they soon become changed people. This is all part of Christ's own words: "Ye must be born again" (John 3:7, KJV).

Even among those who say that they have made room in their hearts for Jesus there are those who are fakers. Some of them are excellent at playing out their roles: they have to be; their lives hang in the balance. To be on guard, we constantly screen the men. One of the most helpless feelings I have ever had came when we decided to dismiss four men on the same day. Outwardly, they appeared to be sincere. Inwardly, we knew they were playing games. They were what we refer to as "jailhouse converts," the kind who can quickly fall into the routine and pick up the jargon of any environment they are thrown into. It is the same way with inmates in jail: they have to learn the routine and the language—the ins and outs—if they are going to survive and be accepted. Addicts of this breed come in to fatten up and to gain physical strength at our expense. They join with us so that they can partake of the fishes and loaves and nothing more. Even so, we want to give these men and women every possible break, for we know that if we turn them out the odds are that they will return to drugs.

I have often stood in the pulpit in our chapel and told the men and women in our program that we want them either to be sincere about Christ or to leave the Center quietly. "Don't toy with God," I tell them. "Unless you get right with God, He is going to expose you as a phony and then you are going to look and feel very foolish. This is God's house and you either have to commit yourself to Him fully or make room for those who are willing to do so. If you are lingering here for some selfish reason, then it would be better if you had never heard the gospel at all."

If this sounds like rather harsh language, it is intended to be so. We have found that a direct, no-nonsense approach is the only kind of talk that gets through to these people.

Within a few weeks after having moved to the Center I was so absorbed in my work that I frequently lost track of time. When I would hear or see people heading for the cafeteria I would have to ask myself, "Is it time for lunch or supper? Let's see, it must be supper, because we had hot dogs for lunch. No, that was yesterday. Or was it?" My only solution was to check the clock. And there were days when I would even have trouble remembering the date—not whether it was the 17th or the 18th, but whether it was January or February. Worst of all was the fact that I had so little time to spend with Cindy. I would often start work at eight or nine in the morning and not get back to our apartment until midnight or the wee hours of the next day.

With each passing month, Dave spent more and more time away from the office telling people about our work, asking for their prayers and trying to raise funds to keep us going. My anxiety seemed to increase in direct proportion to the number of days that Dave was away. I could feel the pressures pyramiding; the more I tried to dig in and hold my ground the more I found myself sinking deeper into the quicksand of frustration.

Upon returning from his trips Dave would always come bouncing into the office and ask me, "How're things going?" If I was in quicksand only up to my knees, I would reply, "Good." If the quicksand was up to my neck, I would say, "Pretty good." I was determined not to complain unduly, feeling that I would be portraying manliness by swallowing my woes. Dave quickly saw through me, deciphering the difference between "Good" and "Pretty Good" and letting me know that there was no shame in having problems. He made his shoulder available for me to lay the burdens of the work upon. As head man not only did Dave want to know about what was happening, he was entitled to know all the details—the acid-coated ones as well as the sugar-coated ones. When we were engaged in discussions of this type I felt particularly close to Dave. Alas, those moments when we were able to share our troubles and pray together about them were becoming fewer and fewer.

six /...
···/ where there's smoke,
/ there's a liar

IT DIDN'T TAKE LONG for the sleepless nights to set in. Even when I would get home early and the night would pass without alarms, I would lie awake anticipating problems. Before long, my days became as exasperating as my nights. I became so emotionally involved in the struggles of each addict that whenever one would stray from the path of progress I would get upset. If one walked out on us, I would blame myself, slumping into an attitude of disgust for days at a time. When I was locked in such deplorable corridors of time, my appetite would vanish and my heart would ache so that I felt it was going to burst through my chest. Each time this kind of crisis would occur, it was a foregone conclusion that my nights were going to be ceiling-gazers. In my attempts to rise above the circumstances I vowed to try all the harder. To me that meant staying even longer at night at 416 to help prevent addicts from giving in to temptation and walking out on us.

The next stage was, I suppose, inevitable. I began to search for reasons why everything wasn't operating 100 percent the way I felt it should. More than anything, I sought out someone to whom I could transfer the blame, although I wasn't aware at the time that this was what I was doing. My focus became fixed on Dave. "If he had been here, Pedro would never have left," I would tell myself. "Dave doesn't have to travel *that* much. He's out there having a good time and I'm back here doing the work that belongs to him. Even when he's here he botches things up. He just doesn't know how to handle addicts because he's not around them enough. That's why, when it comes time to decide how to deal with them, Dave always makes the wrong decisions."

Needless to say, that was an unhealthy attitude to develop. It might not have been so bad had it not gone beyond that level. I was quite upset, however, and I told some of our workers about my feelings concerning Dave. It wasn't long before word filtered back to Dave, whereupon he summoned me to his office. We had a long talk that did both of us a lot of good. More than anything, I wanted him to understand how these tensions of the past few months had been building up. Although it shouldn't have come as a surprise to me, I was left with my mouth agape when Dave told me about the predicaments he had encountered in previous years of building up the ministry. I recognized that he had been through everything that I had faced, and then some. At one point, when Dave became angry with me and lashed out at me verbally, tears filled my eyes. As he spoke to me I remember feeling that the tears weren't there so much because he was giving me a piece of his mind as because I was entering into a new and deeper appreciation for my brother.

In the past there had been more than just the eight-year difference in our ages that had separated us. Dave always had such a positive attitude and had seen so many answers to prayer in recent years that he had built up an indomitable faith. Like other men of such profound faith and vision, Dave was often hard to speak to. I mean this only in a complimentary way, for at that stage of my life I had not yet acquired the degree of spiritual strength that Dave had. My respect for him grew immensely that day because I got an insight into his life and what he had been through. Having watched him all the more closely ever since, I have seen him persevere through periods of almost unendurable stress and oftentimes I have fallen to my knees in prayer to thank God for having upheld Dave.

Nevertheless, I was still bogged down by the work. It was so hard to learn how to deal with drug addicts. Unless you have had a chance to work closely with them it is impossible to imagine how warped their lives have become, how animalistic some of them have grown, how immature they are, and how incapable they are of coping with everyday life.

"The addict is basically an infantile personality," says Irwin B. Gould, director of the Drug Addiction Institute at the Post Graduate Center for Mental Health in Manhattan. That might seem like a rather mild statement. It is, however, quite significant when you consider the word "infantile," which helps get across the point that these people really are like infants. What makes the addict such a contentious person to handle is that the infantile personality is housed in a body that is anywhere from thirteen to forty years of age. (Addicts seldom live beyond the age of forty.) At an age when they should be learning how to accept responsibility, these people are as irresponsible as infants. Their lives are bound in on one side by their needs and on the other side by their desires, and what creates the havoc is that both their needs and desires are centered on narcotics.

In the life of every addict who is sincerely attempting to rebuild himself there are multiple problems. After surviving cold turkey, an addict's mind and body begin to change. One of the first realizations he must face is that he is embarking on an entirely new way of living. His values, his habits, his friends, his thoughts, his language are all undergoing a revision. As he examines himself and his new surroundings, he must make many decisions: Is Teen Challenge worth the effort? Does he *really* want to be free of narcotics? The craving for drugs has not yet left him. He has been too long bound in sin to shake it so easily. As he watches reformed addicts around him at the Center he draws encouragement. Each day has its temptations, though. There is always the knowledge that he can walk out of the Center of his own free will any time he chooses and can get that shot of heroin he knows his buddies are getting back in his old neighborhood.

With the darkness come the hardest hours. In many instances it takes two or three weeks before these addicts are able to get a decent night's sleep. Their nerves are taut, their minds hyperactive. This is one reason we try to keep them busy during the day, hoping that the work we have them perform will tire them enough that they will be able to drop off to sleep easily. We know that the night hours are the haunting hours, the time when memories surge in on them from all sides. Some addicts can't take it; they walk out the front door and never come back. Each time one of them goes, I feel that I have lost another personal battle.

We encourage the men to pray, especially when they are upset. In a roundabout way, even prayer has sometimes caused problems, however. Some addicts get so involved in their night-time prayer in their rooms that they begin shouting, almost as if they believe God is deaf in one ear so that they must yell in order to be heard. We don't mind fervent prayer, but when it gets so loud that other addicts cannot sleep, then something has to be done. Some of these vociferous prayer-warriors don't quite understand why we want them to quiet down. They feel that using this sacred privilege in such an earnest endeavor should not bother anyone. Others can't figure us out: first we urge them to pray and then when they do so, we come along and tell them to quiet down. We point out that this is precisely what we want them to do, to quiet down, not to shut up. In recent years we have been pleased to see that the addicts who share a room together will often share a period of quiet prayer before going to bed. One of their most frequent prayers is that God will free them of the torment of the night—the temptations, the thoughts and the dreams that cause them to toss, turn and scream.

A lesson we had to learn very early was that going through cold turkey was only the *first* step on the way to recovery. All of us had tended to give these people too much credit for abstaining from narcotics for a few days, perhaps because of the compassion we felt from having witnessed the ordeal they had passed through. It took a number of painful experiences for us to understand that withdrawal from drugs for such a short period was merely the beginning of the building of a new life.

As soon as the addicts got an inkling that we were willing to trust them, they often took advantage of us. One of the most serious problems we used to have was with thievery. One enterprising fellow made full use of the freedom we had been allowing him; he went back to the dormitory at 416, tied some bedsheets together, then lowered a typewriter out the window. Next, he went downstairs, walked around to the back of the building, untied the typewriter from the sheets and took off. Sometimes the men steal from each other. Remembering how often they themselves used to filch things, the victims generally take such losses philosophically, reasoning that they might well have done the same to someone else. Now we constantly change the locks on doors in an effort to remove this temptation.

Some of their shenanigans struck closer to home—my home. Eddie and Ruth, a man and wife who had been in our program, decided to cut out one night and on their way they swiped our baby stroller. (We had been blessed with a daughter, Kristie.) Those were the days when the addicts also found me a pretty easy mark in another way. They would come up to me with tales of woe in an effort to gain my permission to leave the Center for a few hours or for a night. I fell for their line the first time that one of them put on an Oscar-winning performance to convince me that his mother was ill or that his aunt or uncle had died. To make matters worse, I believed those stories when I heard them for the second and third and fourth times. Then, after doing a little quick mathematics, I calculated that at the rate that aunts and uncles were passing away the population of New York would be cut in half within a few more months. I was chagrined to think that I had been taken in so easily, but my embarrassment turned to anger when I discovered that these men I had been giving liberty to had been using their free time to go out and shoot up with drugs.

In recent years, there has been a tightening up on the liberties granted to addicts and we have found that they appreciate this. It seems that they feel more secure knowing that we are more aware of what is going on and that we cannot be so easily duped.

Perhaps the most frequently violated rule at Teen Challenge is the one which forbids all smoking. Those who try to get away with smoking haven't counted on me. In all modesty, I must admit that I have to rank myself as one of the world's best at catching sneaky smokers. I can small smoke on a man's breath all the way across a room. At least that is what some of the addicts have decided. The truth is that all I have to do is to stand a little closer than usual to someone while I am talking to him, which I often do if I suspect him, and if he has been smoking I can detect it instantly. Those who know of my prowess frequently will raise their hands when they see me

coming and they will say, "Honest, I haven't been smoking."
They won't come right out and admit their guilt, but when
they try to hide from me then I know what's going on—I know
that where there's smoke there's a liar. When they see me zeroing in on them, though, they relent and say, "Yeah, I had a
cigarette. I'm sorry."

After I have given them a warning against breaking the no-
smoking rule again, I like to finish up by telling them, "Not
only am I a minister, but I am a member of the Cancer Society
as well. More people are dying as the result of cigarette smoking than from overdoses of drugs. You came here to get a fresh
start on life. Don't spoil it by endangering your life in this
way."

Once in a great while someone will smuggle in some drugs
to the Center. We have even caught addicts bringing in small
cellophane bags of heroin in their mouth. Incidents such as this
are becoming less and less frequent, thanks to the fact that the
converted addicts on our staff are well aware of all the tricks
and can quickly spot anyone who has taken any narcotics or
who is trying to bring some in.

Little by little we have been getting smarter. Now that we
have tightened our security, have required verification of an
illness or death in the family before letting someone go home,
and have been able to cut down on smoking and smuggling,
we have had less and less trouble.

As hard as we try and as much as we have been able to im-
prove our methods, there are some occurrences that are beyond
our control. I am thinking right now of one case in particular
involving one of our older addicts, a man named Tony, whom
temptation seemed to approach from all angles. Listen to his
story:

"This one guy says to me, 'Come on, let's get out of the
Center for a couple hours. I know where we can get some
dope.'

" 'Wait,' I told him. 'I don't have any money.'

" 'Look,' he says, 'I know where they keep the keys to
the vehicles and the brown one's right out back. Don't worry
about money.'

" 'No,' I told him. 'I can't go.'

"I let it go at that and the next thing I knew this guy had taken off, just took the vehicle and went. He went back to his neighborhood and he took guys over to New York in the vehicle. They copped some drugs and this is how he got his fix. He didn't get away with it, though. He brought the car back that night, but by then the detectives were lookin' for him.

"I didn't go with the first guy, but when another guy named Broadway Jake came up with a Thunderbird one day it was even harder to resist. I wasn't really set on staying at Teen Challenge anyway so I went with him. When I came back to the Center, Don had to find out if he could trust me this time. He made me show up each day and sit in the lobby and go to classes and go to chapel. Then he sent me back out into the streets again. After a whole week of that he said, 'Okay, Tony, you can come back in and rejoin us.'

"From then on I stayed. The only thing I'm sorry about is that I didn't come to the Lord a long, long time ago. The first time I came to Teen Challenge I was livin' in the flophouses down on the Bowery, payin' a buck ten a night. I was separated from my wife. She didn't want no part of me then. We were separated for as long as I was on drugs, which was about three and a half years. It took about eight months after I came to the Lord before my wife came back to me. She kept saying, 'Tony, you told me too many times you was off it.' Then one day she said, 'Tony, I'm seein' that what you have now is real and I have to admit that this time I believe you're going to make it.' "

seven /...
···/ the ultimate weapon—
/ prayer

W HAT TIME will you be home for supper?" Cindy would ask as I would leave for work in the morning.

"I have no idea," I would tell her. "You know as well as I do that too many things happen and that I can't make any promises. Maybe I'll be home at 6 o'clock. Maybe I'll be home at 3 in the morning. What more can I tell you?"

I couldn't blame Cindy for asking me. She was becoming almost as overwrought by our situation as I was. Instead of getting better, things were getting worse. Finances at Teen Challenge were so low that there were many days when we weren't sure where we would get the money to pay for the next meal for all the people at the Center. When we did have food, it was often poorly prepared. We were badly understaffed, our men's dormitory was overcrowded, and we were unable to find anyone who could cope with the female addicts. In addition to all that, paper work piled up to Matterhorn proportions during Dave's absences. He was gone for longer and longer stretches—occasionally for a solid month—and our conversations were reduced to long-distance telephone calls and to infrequent face-to-face visits. Decisions which I had been formerly able to leave for Dave to make when he got back from a trip now became my responsibility. I felt the ultimate weight of decision-making: fretting about what choices should be made and then continuing to worry about them once I had made them. When I finally would get to bed at night, I became a pillow-wrestler. I spent long hours staring into the darkness. When I slept, it must have been fitfully, because when I got up to go to work

I didn't feel rested. I began to look as bad as I felt. Even when I am in the best of health, my physical dimensions make me resemble a six-foot tall pencil, but one day I got a real jolt when I looked in the mirror. Just to make certain of what I saw, I looked a little more closely and then finally had to admit to myself, "You're not there. There's no 'you' in that mirror. You have become so thin that you don't even exist any longer."

My health was being ruined, my married life was being constantly intruded upon by the demands of the work, and my outlook in general had reached an all-time low. Gone was the glamor of the work. Also missing now was the fervor with which I had approached my duties in days past. Clearly, something had to be done. What I decided to do was quit.

Once I had made up my mind to leave, the only thing I had to figure out was how to go about resigning. I couldn't make up my mind whether to drop Dave a note about it or whether I should wait until he returned to the office and then boldly march in and tell him, "I've had enough of this nonsense. I quit." To cover myself from all angles, I wrote out a letter of resignation and also rehearsed a forceful speech. Now all I had to do was sit back and wait for Dave to show up.

One of the things that had motivated me to resign was that Mom kept dropping hints that maybe I should leave. She was well aware that I was not standing up too well under the burdens of my new job and she used to say to me, "Don't you think you'd better go back to pastoring? Maybe this is not the work God wants you to be in." Mom, who had been so right so often, was trying to be kind, and thinking about her words made me wonder if it might not be best for all concerned if I did leave. After one unusually trying day, I decided that, yes indeed, God did *not* want me at Teen Challenge any longer.

In what seemed to me to be a strange turn of emotions, I sensed that I had no feeling of relief about quitting. I couldn't help wondering why this was so. Something was amiss and I wanted to know what it was. I knew that there was only one way to find out what was happening, so I went into the bedroom, closed the door and began praying. That next hour or so may well have been the most important of my life, resulting as it did in a new and fuller relationship with the Lord. God taught me so much during that period of prayer that the repercussions of His conversation with me have been felt in every area of my existence since then—in the tiniest niches of my life, in the deepest recesses of my soul, in the broad and sweeping panorama of today, tomorrow and eternity.

I am not trying to be melodramatic. There is no need to be. What God did for me during those hours of prayer was simply to give me a good lesson in anatomy: He shook me by my heels, extracted my foot from my complaining mouth, set my eyes upon Him, opened my ears to reality, pointed my nose straight ahead and reminded me that my progress would be swifter if I would get down on my knees more often in prayer.

My prayer life had been deteriorating during the past year or so; that, more than anything else, was why my days had become so saturated with anxiety and so devoid of happiness. How could I have bungled things so badly? How could I have been negligent in prayer, in Bible study, and in my walk with the Lord? Hold it—as soon as these thoughts entered my mind I dismissed them, realizing that dwelling on such negative thoughts had had much to do with my earlier downfall. After all, I had always been in prayer and study and had tried to be led by the Lord, but now I knew that I had not let Him do the leading in these things and that I had tried to accomplish too much on my own. Now, with my feet, eyes, ears, nose and knees all prepared to function as they should, I was ready to go to work.

Exactly what transpired during my long prayer session? Well, the first thing I asked God for was permission to leave Teen Challenge, for an indication of His approval and for a sense of relief in my own mind that I was making the right move. And the first thing that God pointed out to me during our prayer-conversation was that I was a quitter. He made clear to me the difference between quitting (which was a form of running away that I was attempting) and leaving (which would have been permissible had the Lord set up another field of work for me to enter). That, like most of what I learned that day, was not a profound lesson. To me, though, it was an important one.

It was also vital for me to recognize that I was causing most of my own headaches because I had not been approaching each hurdle with a Christian stride. God showed me that I was behaving much like the man, who, when asked "How are you doing?" replied, "Oh, pretty well, under the circumstances." My trouble was that I was *under* the circumstances instead of using God's strength to climb above them.

Something else that was revealed to me that day was that I had a position of responsibility and that people were depending on me, some even entrusting their lives into my care. God now impressed upon me the need to see what an opportunity I had to be of service to hundreds of men and women if I could harness my talents. To do this meant that my own spiritual growth would have to be as dynamic as that of Teen Challenge itself. I felt that God was taking the blinders off my eyes so that I would see that He wanted me to remain at the Center and to rededicate myself to the work and into His keeping. For about a year now I had been trying to do things through my own strength; in the process I had fouled things up as badly as a kitten playing with a ball of yarn. Oh, Teen Challenge had been moving forward in spite of me, but I was getting in my own way so much that I had become my own worst enemy. When I took time out to pray and to be honest with God, He made it clear that we would have to tackle the job at the Center together. And that is the sort of relationship I have tried to maintain ever since, working as hard as I possibly can, but remembering always to bring my needs to God, to leave them there and then sit back and watch Him perform the impossible.

One of the best indicators that I had undergone a change for the good came a few days after my unusual prayer session.

"What time will you be home for supper?" Cindy asked as I left for work.

"I have no idea," I began.

"Please give me *some* idea of when you'll be back. Don't tell me you have to stay late again tonight. You don't have to spend all those hours there."

I was all set to launch into my usual dissertation on how important it was for *me* to be at 416 when I suddenly remembered not to stick my foot in my mouth. Cindy knew as well as I did that my presence at 416 helped only to a limited degree and that there had been a number of occasions when I had tried to talk men out of leaving and had failed. I think we both knew that there was going to be no stopping some of these people, no matter how many hours I spent at 416. One of my fears about coming home was that I was always apprehensive about reporting back in the morning and finding that someone had left the Center in the dark of the night. On this particular morning as I stood before Cindy, I knew that she was right and that it was time for me to entrust this burden to the Lord by means of some earnest prayer.

"I'll be home at six," I told Cindy as I gave her a goodbye kiss.

Praying for the safekeeping of the addicts during the night, I soon learned, was more effective than my mere presence at 416. Seeing that this was the case, I prayed one day, "God, from now on you are the night watchman."

As I began to scrutinize myself more closely, I saw another of my faults. Like so many others, it had arisen because I had felt impulsively that I had to be in the center of everything. Now I saw that my own desire to lead these addicts to salvation and to help them grow spiritually had been detrimental to some of them. In my own overzealous way I had tried to supply their every need and, as a result, I had taught these men to rely on me when they should have been leaning on God. The Lord made me aware of this in a unique way. An addict named Joe used to be in and out of Teen Challenge like a train at Grand Central. Every few weeks Joe would take off for a day or so and whenever he came back he always came to me with the same line: "Brother Don, I came back because of you." I think Joe could see my ego puff up like a balloon, a reaction that spurred him on to say, "You're the only one who really cares for me. I've got a lot of confidence that you can help me. Will you give me another chance?" He was so convincing that I almost longed for him to run away so that he could come back and give my sagging ego a boost. When God opened my eyes to what was going on, I knew that I was hurting Joe more than I was helping him, and that Joe was doing the same to me.

After confessing my mishandling of this situation to God, I called Joe in, explained to him that he would henceforth have to depend on the Lord and not on me. Once the matter was thus resolved we came up with a perfect score: Joe quit fooling around and rid himself of his drug habit; my ego shrank to more normal proportions and thereafter proved to be no hindrance; and God knew that we were now being honest with Him.

Now that God had made me aware that my own spiritual growth was vital to the growth of Teen Challenge, I could see that much of the time I had spent during the past year in prayer and Bible study had been to little avail because I had been taking part only on a superficial level. I had been so preoccupied with the complexities of my work that I had lost my sense of direction, often taking personal offense when a new problem would arise, but then trying to solve it by giving more and more of myself to the job. That was all quickly becoming a part of the past. Every time I noticed one of my flaws, I set about to correct it. I wasn't able to repair myself completely overnight, but I tried earnestly to seek God's help in making me a more usable servant of His. Little by little I could see evidence that things were getting better. I was learning, like a boxer, to roll with the punches.

If someone were to ask me what the single most important factor has been in the progress of Teen Challenge, I would not have to hesitate before giving a one-word answer: prayer. After spending a few days at the Center, one girl said to me, "All you people do here is sleep, eat and pray. You pray in the morning, you pray at noon, and you pray in the evening." Many of our workers—and this includes Bible school students, longtime Christians and others—have told us that they had done more praying while at the Center than at any other time of their life. One of them summed it up by saying, "We have God in the morning, Jesus Christ in the afternoon, and the Holy Spirit at night."

It was prayer that sent my brother to New York when he heard about the boys who were on trial in the Michael Farmer case and it was prayer that carried him through times of misfortune. These prayers were not only being said by Dave,

but by multitudes of others: his wife, Mom and Dad, his par-
ishioners in Philipsburg, Pennsylvania, and countless other
people. And prayer saved my career at Teen Challenge.

There is no way of knowing which prayers or whose prayers
are being answered sometimes, and it is a good thing that this
is so. It strengthens one's faith in God to see answers to prayer,
and it is rewarding to know that often these replies have come
in response to the prayers of other men and women. Precisely
how prayer can be so effective is something I do not know; my
lack of comprehension merely causes me to thank God that
He is the one who has devised this system and not I. It reminds
me somewhat of the story about Marconi, who, when he was
congratulated by a companion for his invention of the radio,
said, "Thank you, my friend. I just wish I understood what
really made this instrument capable of doing what it does."

So, too, the power of prayer remains, for the most part, a
mystery. There is no way that I can give a definitive explanation of how prayer has become such an effective tool for us. I
can only say that I am constantly learning about its effectiveness. It has been our experience that prayer is one of our most
potent weapons. Sometimes when persons we had been dealing
with or trying to deal with paid no attention to us, we chalked
them off as lost causes. Then we began to revive our efforts on
behalf of these people by praying for them *after* we had lost
direct contact with them. (These are our "never-too-late"
prayers which we began using by asking God to work in the
lives of these men and women and to send them to us so that
we might be able to help them.) It wasn't long before we began getting news from members of our staff who had been trying out the never-too-late prayers that the very people they had
been praying about had come to Teen Challenge of their own
volition. More often than not, those who came said they came
out of a feeling of compulsion rather than out of any desire of
their own.

As a means of reaching people, prayer will not take the
place of personally going out and witnessing to them, but we
have discovered that it is a valuable adjunct to our ministry.
Another lesson we have been taught is that prayers are not always answered quickly and that we must be faithful in bringing

our petitions to God time after time until we have had a response to them.

In my instructions to our staff members, I tell them one of the worst mistakes they can make is to become emotionally involved with any of the people in our program. I tell them that it is imperative that they always maintain a safe distance from the patients. By this I don't mean a physical distance, but rather the gap that must be retained between teacher and pupil or counselor and patient. We keep a sharp watch to make certain that no one becomes a teacher's pet and that there is no buddy-buddy relationship between a worker and a patient. It has been our experience that such relationships are harmful to both sides.

One of the biggest dangers of such a closeness is the painful reaction suffered by the staffer who has become emotionally involved with a patient who goes into a slump or leaves the Center. It is a natural tendency for the worker to blame himself. I have seen workers who have been sent reeling by such cases. Over and over they ask, "What did I do wrong? What did I do wrong?" I know how they feel, for I was a victim of such an episode and I too spent long hours questioning and blaming myself.

There is no way to prepare for such shocks, no way of knowing who might be the next one to leave. We have had cases where we have worked with boys who seemed to be doing exceptionally well and then all of a sudden—poof—something would happen and they would disappear. Experience has taught us that all our self-pity and all our sorrow about these situations is worthless.

There is something that we can do, however, when we are faced with such occurrences. Instead of moping around, we resort to our never-too-late prayers. I tell our staff members, "That fellow who ran away needs your help and there is nothing more helpful that you can do than to pray for him." Dozens of times we have had patients return to us who have told us that they felt they were being pulled back to the Center against their own desires.

eight /...
···/ the door swings
/ both ways

B EING A MERE MORTAL, I did not get straight A's on my report card in the days immediately following my momentous prayer session. There was just too much of me spread around in too many corners of Teen Challenge to be taken care of all at once. Don't get me wrong—I tried hard. Even so, I couldn't quite shake one of my worst habits. I'd be all right for a day or so and then one afternoon I'd settle back behind my desk, reach into my shirt pocket for my pen so that I could make a few notations—and then I'd freeze. That black pen I had in my hand—it wasn't mine. Nor was the green one, nor the gold job, nor were the two mechanical pencils mine. Not even the purple and orange thing from Klutz's Superior Bologna. I counted them: one, two, three, four, five, six. Somehow during the past few hours I had—(a) stolen, (b) borrowed, (c) accidentally taken—four pens and two pencils from people throughout the office. And just when I thought I had kicked the habit.

Had that been my only concern, we would have been in good shape. Although I was approaching my work with more confidence and had made quite a few improvements in our program, there was a limit to what I could do. We were still understaffed and overcrowded. By this time our little dining room at 416 was so overpopulated at mealtime that every seat was taken both at the tables and on the benches that now lined the hallway. Worst of all, people were now also seated on the first half-dozen steps of the staircase, food trays perched precariously on their laps. During the summer, when the addition

78

of college helpers swelled the total population at the Center to seventy-five, the situation became almost intolerable. The ones who had it the hardest were the members of the kitchen staff. Half a dozen or so men scurried around in a one-family kitchen trying to prepare meals for the equivalent of fifteen average-size families.

"Just look at. that," I said to Dave one night. "We can't go on like this."

"I'm as aware of the problem as you are," he told me. "The Lord knows about our problem, too. I've been up late at night in prayer."

Despite these crowded conditions, I was thankful that things were no worse, especially since there was a superabundance of other needs that had to be met. Drug addicts have many physical problems, some of which they are not even aware of. They can see and feel the body sores to which they have become so accustomed, but most of them are surprised to learn that their teeth are in terrible shape. Because they spend so much time under the influence of narcotics, which not only make them high but also serve as pain killers, they can easily remain oblivious to their dental problems and other ailments.

Caring for the medical and dental needs of our addict-guests at Teen Challenge is one of our biggest chores. One doctor has volunteered to care for a number of our men and we take a few patients to him. For the most part, though, we take the addicts to the clinic at nearby Cumberland Hospital.

The person who has just withdrawn from the depths of sin and who is now exploring an entirely new way of life faces demanding days. Every aspect of his life is in transition. No longer does he have to worry about getting a fix, or committing a robbery so that he will have enough money to pay for his drugs. No longer does he have to worry about where he will sleep or eat. And no longer does he have to look with distrust and fear as he surveys everyone who is a part of his daily life.

We appreciate all that the patient is going through and we try to hurry him along the way to complete recovery. Some may feel that we make too much haste, but we have found it imperative for most addicts to be kept busy, to have their minds and bodies on the go. When each day is made meaningful, they can all look back upon it knowing that they have learned, improved and grown stronger.

Since it is only natural that addicts should want to return to their family, friends and neighborhood, they find it hard to believe when we tell them that it will be some two or three months before we will allow them to leave the Center without supervision. Then, depending upon their home situation and their own spiritual growth and physical strength, we will allow them to leave for no longer than a day or, at the most, a weekend. We tell them that we are beginning to trust them, but that we don't trust the devil, who is trying to lure them. Our records show that 90 percent of those who leave without permission go back to the needle.

It is so hard for them to realize how weak they are. They are proud of having gone through cold turkey and they feel that the fact that they had enough will power to survive that is proof that they can get through any situation. The best indication of how lacking in strength they are is that they cannot yet see their own weaknesses.

No matter how the people come to us—either because of our street corner ministry, our literature, or because someone else sent them—they soon find out what Teen Challenge is all about. We do not drum into them day after day the belief that they are going to have a hard time overcoming their problems or that they are wretched and despicable men and women. And we *never* tell a drug addict, "Once an addict, always an addict." On the contrary, we attack their cases with optimism; not with our own optimism, but with that which we have gained from God.

One man, who had tried all the cures and had not achieved any satisfaction, finally decided that he knew how to put an end to his dependence on drugs. For some unexplainable reason he felt certain that burning the needle marks from his arms would be his panacea. That's precisely what he tried to do, heating a frying pan on the stove until it was red hot, then applying the pan to the needle marks. The stench of seared flesh filled the room, and the agony of his self-inflicted cure drove him screaming out to the street. When he regained his senses, he noticed the welts on his arms. He also noticed that his longing for narcotics had not diminished even to the slightest extent.

This is only a small portion of the story of the struggles of Louie, who later came to Teen Challenge for help. After being with us for several days, Louie decided that as much as he wanted to be free of drugs he simply could not live without them. No amount of counseling on our part could dissuade him from his course, and it was with deep sadness that we saw Louie walk out of our door. He walked a couple of blocks to the subway, where he planned on getting a train that would take him back to his neighborhood. As he started down the steps to the subway, Louie paused. To himself he prayed, "God, if you are real, make yourself known unto me *right now*." There is no way of knowing what transpires in the heart of a man, but somehow, right there on those subway steps, Louie suddenly gained a realization of God and understood what we had been trying for days to get across to him. Louie walked back up the steps, retraced his path to Teen Challenge, and walked through our doors, never to walk out on us again.

Simon was another who was all set to leave. As I walked out of the Center and headed for home one night, Simon came running up to me. "Brother Don," he began, "I'm leaving and I just wanted to thank you for trying to help me."

He walked beside me down Clinton Avenue. As I glanced at the shopping bag Simon was carrying, I could see that he was serious about what he had said, for it contained what few possessions he owned. When I tried to talk him out of such a move, Simon said, "I know I'm a fool for going, but I just can't make it here. This program is not for me. I don't know what I'm going to do. I've got a five-year sentence facing me in court in a couple weeks, but I'm still leaving." With that, Simon turned and walked off.

Later that night, I was back at the Center and, much to my surprise and delight, so was Simon. "I changed my mind," he said. "Is that okay?" The smile on Simon's face was rivaled only by the smile on my own.

Victor also thought about leaving. He didn't tell me so, but I could see by the look on his face what was on his mind. I have become accustomed to this look, so I walked over to him, placed a Bible in his hand and said, "Try reading this." Victor glanced at a few pages, then closed the Bible. He looked at me for a second and then, when he could tell that I had seen the tears in his eyes, he put his head down.

Victor then walked into the chapel, knelt in the middle of the floor and clasped his hands together. "God," he said in a loud voice, "if you *are* real, Jesus Christ, if it *is* true what these people say about you, I want to have it. Please. Please, God, change me; take this desire for drugs from me. Be real to me. I'm tired of hospitals. I'm tired of hurting my parents. I'm tired of life. I want to change, but I don't know how."

When Victor walked out of the chapel he was a new man. Never again did he think about leaving the Center. As he has told me several times since then, "I know that we can't always go by feelings, but I felt something that day that changed my life. Jesus Christ took all the desire for drugs away and put a new desire there to serve Him." Victor's desire was such that he became our first missionary, working for Teen Challenge in South America.

Many of those who go out the door never come back. A few have been gone for several days or weeks before coming back to us. One of those who left for nearly a week explained why he returned by saying, "You can't fully appreciate the presence of God until you have gone back out into the presence of Satan." Another summed it up this way: "I just couldn't enjoy my drugs anymore, not after having been with Jesus." And a young girl told us that, "I felt happy when I came outside and went back to the streets, but when I knew that I had walked out on the Lord I felt miserable."

Gregory was another one who thought about going out the door. I had taken a strong interest in him for a number of reasons. To begin with, Gregory was a Negro who had come to us during the time of some of the worst riots in the Bedford-Stuyvesant area, where he had been living. Since this section is just a few blocks from our Center, I felt that if Gregory could find a solution to his problems at Teen Challenge then others from that neighborhood might be encouraged to come to us too. We had done a lot of praying for Gregory, knowing that his short stay with us had not yet been productive. It was unfortunate that at the time he was with us there happened to be several boys at the Center from the deep South, one of whom had made things rather difficult for Gregory.

All our efforts seemed to have been in vain, though, for one day Gregory came to me and said, "I can't make it here. I haven't made any progress here and I don't feel the Lord has done anything for me. It's time for me to go." I knew Gregory had sincerely been trying.

"Give God one more chance," I said. "If you go into the chapel with me and pray, I guarantee you that God will do something for you."

As soon as we got to the chapel, I prayed for Gregory, asking God to come to his rescue at that very moment. Gregory didn't stir, didn't say a word. I thought to myself, "Don, now you've really put God on the spot. You promised Gregory that something would happen." I closed my eyes and prayed a little longer. Still, Gregory did not react in any way at all. I began to think that perhaps I had overstepped my bounds by insisting that God would take hold of him. Then I looked at Gregory and I saw the tears rolling down his face. Turing my head a little further, I saw that tears were spilling from his face onto the chair on which he sat. He began to sob. Then he began to pray out loud. When he arose, he told me, "I feel that the Lord has touched me." During the remainder of his days at the Center, it was evident that the Lord *had* touched Gregory and it was a pleasure to watch him grow in Christian stature.

When some people hear stories such as these, they tend to poke a finger at Christianity and decry the tears and the emotionalism and happy endings. That, I assure you, is because they don't know what they are poking a finger at. We place absolutely no emphasis on tears or emotionalism at Teen Challenge; whatever weeping or crying out that takes place comes from the hearts of men who would have sworn they would never have been caught dead praying or sobbing. Louie, Simon, Victor and Gregory were not fairy-tale characters I created. These men were once finger-pokers themselves. When they came to Teen Challenge they were hardened men who wouldn't flinch at the prospect of belting you over the head if they felt you had money they could steal and buy drugs with.

These are the hard-core men with long police records, men who have spent years in jail, men who have been gangster-tough. Try poking a finger at them and telling them that Christianity is a song-and-dance routine, the easy way out. Or, better yet, try accepting Christ into your own life if you have not done so. It takes guts, doesn't it? These men, who had enough nerve to commit robberies every day of the week, found that it took more courage to be a Christian than to be a burglar, more guts to admit their needs and to ask Christ to take over their lives.

The chapel is the hub of our activity at Teen Challenge. We begin the day there in prayer and song and we end the day there in prayer and song. Two of our converts got a bit carried away with their prayers one evening. They had gone to the chapel because they had felt the need to be alone with God. The evening chapel service was to start at 7:30, but we respected the needs of these men and, consequently, waited until they had finished. By the time they had concluded their prayers it was 9 P.M.

There are always quite a few Spanish-speaking people at the Center and shortly before chapel services begin they start calling out, "Capilla. Capilla." That is a Spanish word meaning "chapel," and it has been used so often that just about everyone says "Capilla" these days.

One of the men came up with a rather unusual, although apt, way of calling the others to chapel. He called out, "Let's go, it's medication time." How true this has been, for many people have had their needs taken care of in chapel—needs that had not been relieved by hospitals, doctors, psychiatrists or pills.

Dave and I are ministers in the Assemblies of God, which is a Pentecostal denomination. Some people have told us that we are a noisy group during our church services. We are, undeniably, louder than most church groups. It is not our intent, however, to place a premium on noise. We simply believe that the most effective type of prayer is the most spontaneous and uninhibited kind. When Peter was walking upon the water and began to sink, he "cried out, saying, Lord, save me." (Matthew 14:30, KJV).

There are a lot of people in our chapel services who, knowing that they are sinking fast, ask for help from God in the manner of Peter, crying out with plenty of volume. And there are those who, having accepted God's gift of salvation, cry out because of the zeal and joy that has come over them. Our singing is also rather spirited. In our old chapel we had to open the windows wide to get air; the sounds that wafted through the neighborhood when we were conducting our services were not always well received.

One night, some of the neighbors called the police. When the sergeant and his righthand man walked into 416 that night and demanded to know what was going on, one of our staffers tried to explain:

"Well, you just go right in there and tell them to stop making all that noise," the sergeant instructed our worker.

"I can't very well do that," said our man. "That's not plain noise they're making. That's praying and the people who are doing the praying are reformed drug addicts, alcoholics, prostitutes and gang members. We've taught them to pray, so I can't just go in there now and tell them to disregard all that we have told them about the importance of prayer."

"Okay, then I'll go in and stop it," said the sergeant, forcefully. He opened the door to the chapel, walked inside and was flabbergasted to see people on their knees praying and crying. A minute later, the sergeant gingerly slipped out of the chapel and closed the door. He cleared his throat, looked at his partner and said, "*You* go in and stop it."

Dutifully, the young patrolman took his turn at going into the chapel, but whatever determination he had to restore quiet was melted in an instant as he gazed around the room. A minute later he, too, was softly closing the chapel door behind him as he left. When he looked at the sergeant, he shrugged his shoulders. Then the two of them got back in their patrol car and drove off.

Our chapel has been the scene of some of the most memorable events of my life, and I know that this is true of thousands of other people as well. There are times when I am speaking during a chapel service that I feel almost overwhelmed by a combination of compassion for those who are yet unsaved and by love for those who have been. Sometimes I look at these men and women and I think that there are a few who obviously are hopeless cases. At moments such as this I like to remember Tom. One of our workers had this to write about him:

"He had been a head accountant at a hospital in Brooklyn until six months ago. His problem had started eight years before with 'social' drinking. On Sunday, September 1, Tom, a drunkard, was brought to the Center by a former high school classmate who had picked him up from a gutter near the King's Avenue Hebrew Mission. He shook with delirium tremens so badly that he could not lie still. They carried him into the chapel, and my heart was stricken as I observed his filthy, shaking, skinny, half-decayed body.

"He was so repulsive that I turned my head away. I asked in my heart, 'God, can you help HIM?' The stench from his body almost overcame me. They got him to a room on the second floor where the fellows held him in their arms and fed him, for he couldn't hold his own spoon. His stomach was weak, and he could hardly hold down the juice and soup that they gave him, but he was all smiles in spite of his shakes."

Three days later, Tom crawled out of bed, raised himself into a kneeling position and asked the Lord to take control of his life and grant him salvation.

nine /...
···/ a walk along
/ clinton avenue

D AVE AND I DID MORE than pray about our need for enlarging
the Center; we put feet and miles to our prayers by in-
vestigating every place we felt might be suitable. What we were
seeking was a spot where we could build a new Center. Our
search began on Staten Island and we nearly jumped up and
clicked our heels the day we came across a spacious lot that
seemed to be ideal. As we scanned the lot we both became
excited at the prospects it offered and before long we were
nervously chattering about our grand plans for every square
inch of space.

"We can have a gymnasium over there," I said, pointing in
one direction. "The ball field would go over there, the main
building would have to be right about there and over in that
corner we could put. . . ." I had to stop and laugh at myself
because I was pointing in so many directions that I felt like
a weather vane in a tornado.

"We can keep an office going in Brooklyn where we can
interview addicts and we can keep 416 as a place for the staff
to live," Dave said when I had slowed down enough to give
him a chance.

"Suburbia," I added. "We would be able to get the fellows
away from Brooklyn and out here where there is air and
where they can see trees. That in itself will help with their
rehabilitation."

From there on, things moved swiftly, with the architect
setting our visions down in blueprints and then building a
scale model of what was to be our new home. Negotiations had

been begun to buy the property and we were awaiting the day when we could sign the papers and start building. Word had been sent to our friends and sponsors that we were soon going to erect new headquarters. Just when all the pieces seemed to be fitting together, though, along came an unexpected gust that blew things apart. What happened was that the land we were after had suddenly and inexplicably been condemned by the local legislators. That was it. That was the end of the vision. Almost, but not quite.

Mom overheard me ask Dave, "What do we do now? Have we failed God in some way that He should punish us like this?"

"I think that you boys simply tried to get a little bit ahead of God," said Mom. Our ears stood at attention.

"Why didn't you tell us we were rushing ahead on our own and not under God's power?" I asked Mom.

"Because you wouldn't have listened anyway," she said.

Nobody bats 1.000, but Mom is right so much of the time that we took her word concerning the matter. As Dave and I talked about the recent events, we saw that we had been trying to handle this big venture on our own and that we had wanted to pick the location rather than have the Lord show it to us. Although neither of us understood why the Lord had let us waste so much time on the Staten Island project, I think both of us fully expected that we would some day have our answer. Next, we began scouring Long Island and when we inspected an estate owned by a former U. S. ambassador we felt that we had found our own Brigadoon.

"Just think of it," I said to Cindy, "no more cement lawns. There's room to roam around in and the air is clean and there are birds."

We were zeroing in on a date when we would be able to take over the estate when—here we go again—something happened. It seems that the people in the town where we were hoping to locate took umbrage at our plans, held a meeting, and informed us that they would oppose any move to bring "that kind of people" into their neighborhood.

As we plodded on from one neighborhood to the next, we encountered much the same resistance: Teen Challenge was not welcome. If a town didn't have a law we would have violated by moving in, then everybody scurried around and wrote up a law lickety-split that would take care of us. Instant laws were our undoing. I couldn't help wondering how those people would have felt toward us if they or one of their loved ones had been in our program trying to kick the drug habit.

Having been stymied on Staten Island and Long Island, we began looking around Manhattan and Brooklyn. Almost daily the realtor would call, blaring into the phone with a voice full of zing, "I've got it. I've got it. I've got another building for you to look at and this time it is *absolutely* the perfect place for you." Early on, Dave and I would be duly aroused, hardly able to wait to get a look at the latest "*absolutely* perfect place." As one discouragement piled atop another, we became less eager to look at places.

"There's not another building in all of New York that we can look at," I said one day. "We've seen them all—hotels, apartment houses, office buildings, churches, gymnasiums, Y.M.C.A.'s—any place that sounded like it might be good for us. They're all either too old, too big, too small, or too dilapidated."

God took us many miles through many months and still we had not found a spot where we could build. It was hard to figure out why it was taking so long. Just about the time we felt we would never find a place, we did—on Clinton Avenue. So often in the past we had felt certain that we knew God's will: Were we right this time? Did He want us to remain in Brooklyn?

I like the way Dave describes what took place after we felt the Lord might want us to stay on Clinton Avenue. His account begins with the day when the two of us, along with Joe Catesi, our treasurer, first looked at buildings on our own block.

"We went down the street and we saw 436, an apartment house. I stood outside and said, 'Lord, you helped us get 416 and now we need you to get 436 for us. I don't know what it will cost, but you know that we have only twenty-five dollars in the treasury.' Then I went up and knocked on the door and asked, 'Who owns this house?' and the man who answered told me, 'The owner's out back.'

"I went back, introduced myself and the owner said, 'Oh, I know you; you're with the drug addicts.'

"I said, 'Yes, and I'd like to buy this house.' He laughed.

" 'Reverend,' he said, 'you may be doing a good work, but I've been remodeling this place. We have thirteen apartments here. My sister and her family just moved in. It's a great income.'

" 'Sir,' I said to him, 'I've been praying to God and asking Him to give me this building.'

"He looked at me and said, 'No, we're not selling. Besides, you couldn't afford the price; I'd want $90,000.'

" 'All right,' I said, 'we'll buy it.' Then I gave him my card and told him, 'We're going back to pray. When you want to call me, just call.' I knew he would call. Two days later I got a telephone call from the man.

" 'Reverend,' he said, 'please come down.'

"I went down with Joe and we were ushered into a big room and introduced to all the members of the family, who were seated in a circle.

" 'Reverend,' said the owner, 'a strange thing happened the other night: my sister got an urge to move to the suburbs. If you can get $90,000, you can have this place.'

" 'You've got a deal,' I said.

"I guess he thought we had $90,000. If only he had known.

"When we got outside, Joe Catesi was shaking his head. 'We don't have $90,000,' he said to me as I stood in front of 444, the building next to 436.

" 'Joe, this is where we're going to build our new Center," I said. "We're going to need this building at 444 and the parking lot behind it so that we'll have enough room.' Then I went up to the door of 444 and knocked. A Negro gentleman came to the door. When I told him we wanted to buy his house he said, 'Reverend, we just bought this place. I just put in a new $4,000 furnace. We're happy here. We're not interested in selling.'

" 'When you feel like calling, here's my card,' I said. I knew he would call, too. It was the next day when he called.

" 'Please come over,' he said.

"I went over with Joe and the man told us, 'You should never have come yesterday. Now my wife wants to move out all of a sudden. Last night we were going all over Brooklyn and the suburbs looking at houses. I'm going to give you one price: $36,000, take it or leave it, plus $3,000 for the furnace.'

"I said, 'I'll buy it.'

"When we got outside, I said to Joe, 'Find out who owns that lot in back of 444 and call the man.' As soon as I got hold of the man on the phone and told him we wanted to buy his lot he said, 'I'm not interested. It's a $20,000 lot and it's a big tax write-off.' After he told me about some more of the benefits he got out of the land, he told me again he wasn't interested in selling it.

" 'Well, sir,' I told him, 'God gave us 436 and 444 and we've got you surrounded. I think you're going to call me back and we're going to get your lot.'

"He called the next day and said, 'You jinxed me. You can have it for $17,000.'

" 'We'll take it,' I said."

Now we owed $90,000 for one house, $36,000 for another, $3,000 for a furnace and $17,000 for a lot, a total of $146,000. Checking our bank balance indicated that we were not penniless; after using all our available funds all we would have left to pay was $145,975. Doubtless, we were shortly going to find out if we had acted according to the Lord's will and if He wanted us to stay on Clinton Avenue. Anxious days were countered with hours of prayer. Everyone at Teen Challenge—secretaries, clerks, counselors, Mom, Dave, all of us and our loved ones—prayed. Within *three weeks* God had supplied the money so that we were able to pay off all the debts on our new properties in cash. In thanks for what He had showed us, all of us bowed our heads in prayer. There were many tear-stained faces and many happy faces, but all were bathed in the utmost sincerity of a people who had witnessed a miracle.

The next few months were like a circus. Come to think of it, we probably would have had an easier time had we borrowed some circus equipment. A trampoline would have been handy in helping us to get over and around each other during those more-crowded-than-ever days. What caused the congestion was that some of us moved into 436 and 444 as soon as we could, there to set up offices and, for some of us, living quarters. That was well enough, but once the workmen got busy at 416 repairing the building, they found they needed room to work. Under pressure from the builders, we had to transfer larger numbers of people to 436, where, before long, life took on that circus-like appearance. People clambered over one another to get to the telephone, their desks, or their beds, all the while dodging carpenters who were too preoccupied with their own tasks to watch where they were walking with their two-by-fours. Our pace was stepped up yet another notch when the painters took over. They must all have been former GIs, believing as they seemed to in the old army slogan, "If it doesn't move, paint it." All of us had to be on our toes and ever on the move lest we wind up having a paint brush applied to our arms, legs or backs. On top of that, 436 was, to put it in plain English, a dirty old building. Cobwebs and spiderwebs hung in profusion. The variety of insects that gamboled throughout 436 would have made the building an entomologist's delight. There were gaping holes in some of the ceilings and a few of the walls sagged so badly that it seemed the only reason they didn't collapse was because they were too lazy.

When all the painting and hammering were done we were able to sit back and enjoy the comforts of our expansion. Our counselors, most of whom had been living at 416 with the addicts, all moved over to 436. Cindy and I wound up with an apartment on the third floor.

During the months of refurbishing, I frequently thought how odd it was that after all our searching the Lord had finally been able to get through to us and show us that the spot He had in mind was right under our noses. It was incongruous. One reason we had not considered staying in Brooklyn was because people on our block had several times circulated petitions in attempts to have us evicted. To our finite way of thinking, there wasn't a chance of trying to convince people who were trying to evict us one day that they should sell their houses to us the next, but God took care of all that and plenty more. No one wanted to sell, yet all of them did once we let the Lord go to work. Raising the necessary money, and doing so in three weeks, was another of those feats that could not have been accomplished without divine intervention. Now, however, came what we might well consider the biggest test of all—the construction of a headquarters building on the site where 444 had once stood, a spacious two-story structure that would cost $500,000. On the day that we decided definitely to plan on such a new Center we had a bank balance of $13.15.

By now the calendar had jumped ahead to late 1965 and the work of Teen Challenge had become known the world over, thanks largely to Dave's first book—*The Cross and the Switchblade*—and to his ministry in hundreds of churches, rallies and crusades from coast to coast and in a number of foreign countries. Thousands of people had taken an interest in helping to support us with regular donations and with their prayers. Dave felt certain that by appealing to these good people and to a number of larger donors he would be able to raise half the money needed for our new Center. Where the other half was to come from we did not know. To the rescue came a gentleman named W. Clement Stone, the president of the Combined Insurance Company of America. Stone gave us a grant of $250,000, without which we would not have been able to construct the new Center at 444 and in gratitude for which we have named the building after him.

I recall many times standing at the window of my office looking out at the construction of 444. Hundreds of people had laughed at our project, some labeling it "a white elephant." Others told us, "You'll never even get the thing started." Then there were those, who, noting that we *had* begun the building, said, "You'll never get it finished." There were times when I almost felt that those in the last group might have been right. Work on the Center was slowed by a steel strike, bad weather and difficulties with the contractors. Never, though, did I give any serious thought that the Center would not be completed; I had too often seen God intervene when causes had seemed hopeless. Anyway, there was too much work to be done, especially since I had decided that it was necessary to update and file correctly our records on all the men, women and

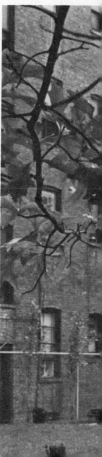

Upper left: No wonder they'd rather play in our yard.
Below: 444 Clinton Avenue, Teen Challenge Center.
Lower left: Chapel services are a high point of every day; here Don is speaking.
Right: "Chow time"—50-70 mouths to feed, a large family.

children who had been a part of the Teen Challenge program. When July of 1967 rolled around, the new Center was finished and we moved into a phase of our ministry in which we no longer had to be constantly concerned about lack of space. All the addicts were now housed in 416, all the counselors and their families in 436.

Perhaps a quick tour through 444 will give you a reasonable mental picture of what it is like. Before we go inside, it is worth pausing for a moment to look at the outside, at its blue and white brickwork and the way the building sprawls across the landscape behind our lawn. Once inside the glass door, we are in our attractive lobby. Off to the right we have enclosed an area where a receptionist now sits. Further back in that corner is a room where addicts are interviewed for possible admission. Off to the left is our new chapel, complete with air conditioning so that our singing and praying won't upset our neighbors. Folding doors at the back of the chapel can be pushed back when necessary so that more people can be seated immediately outside the main chapel. Directly behind the chapel and lobby is a large dining room and kitchen.

Downstairs we have a photographer's darkroom, a recording studio, and a shipping room where we package each month thousands of books, records, copies of our monthly magazine, and tracts about our work. Upstairs is where Mom sits at our small switchboard. There is also a large office for our clerical staff and smaller ones for several of our individual staff members who are in executive positions. On this floor on the left side of the building is a conference room, where staffers often go to take a prayer-break. On the right side is my office. (It actually was Dave's, but he was gone so much and my office got so crowded that I figured he wouldn't mind if I took his.)

Let's go back outside now. A six-foot-high wire fence encircles the lawn in front of our headquarters at 444. That fence was not erected to keep the people in our program *inside;* it was put up to keep the neighborhood children *outside.* Until we learned better, these youngsters used our lawn for a variety of their activities. What made our lawn such an attractive spot for them was that it was the only lawn in the area that was larger than a postage stamp, and they made themselves right at home on it. In other parts of the country this wouldn't be so bad, but in this locale, home is often not the wholesome or neat place that it is elsewhere. Home, for many of the people along Clinton Avenue, is the center of hostility instead of love, of abuse instead of tender care, of filth instead of cleanliness. Thus it was that our lawn soon began to look more like a littered battleground than like the garden spot of America.

Once we had the fence installed, however, the lawn in front of 444 was assaulted from another direction. Angry tenants in the apartment house next door began tossing their garbage on our lawn, some of them throwing bags filled with refuse from the fourth and fifth stories. It seems that we were the target of such barrages because our neighbors were suspicious about our activities until members of our staff visited them to explain what we were doing and invited them to come to our chapel services. Once the word got around that we were trying to help people like themselves, they ceased their garbage-throwing and their attitude changed to one of respect. We were also aided in winning over our neighbors by the large volume of publicity we got. A woman who lived across the street from the Center came over one day, said that she had read about us in *Good Housekeeping,* thought that we were doing a commendable work and handed us a check for $100.

Only a few of the regular residents on the block have been dope users. A few years ago, however, approximately two dozen addicts lived across the street from 416. This was an added burden for the men who were going cold turkey or who, having passed that stage, were straining to remain clean of drugs. If they simply looked across the street they could always be sure of seeing a handful of addicts and pushers milling around. The situation was solved for us by the narcotics squad, which repeatedly raided the building across the street, drove all the addicts out and finally had the place closed down.

All of this might lead you to suspect that Clinton Avenue has now become a haven of serenity where youngsters skip merrily down the street while Mom and Pop sit at home and read. Alas, this is not the way it is. Let's take a stroll down Clinton Avenue and see what it is really like.

Once-attractive apartment houses dominate the block. Clinton Avenue used to be part of a ritzy neighborhood, a street on which socialites lived. Some of the Rockefellers lived on our block years ago and traces of such historic background are part of the heritage of Clinton Avenue. It takes no more than a single glance at the once-proud apartment houses lining both sides of the street to see that the block is no longer a residence for the elite. Scores of shattered windows wear a snaggle-toothed look; at night they shine forth like so many jack-o'-lanterns all in a row. Sidewalks are littered with trash, some of it aimlessly tossed there, some of it spewing out of too-full garbage cans. Here and there a few people lean against the buildings or sit on the front stoops. Others participate in one of Brooklyn's favorite pastimes: sticking their heads out through an open window to engage in loud conversations with friends across the street or on the sidewalk. On the gate of the Galilee Baptist Church across the street from the Center a sign says, NO LOAFING ALLOWED.

Cars line every inch of parking space on both sides of the street. There always are at least a few that have been destroyed either by fire or by energetic hustlers who, during the night, have removed the tires, seats, motors and anything else usable. The reasons for setting cars on fire or looting them are varied. I once saw a girl, in a fit of anger because her boyfriend had jilted her, smash every window of a brand new yellow Cadillac belonging to her erstwhile suitor.

Sitting uneasily in a puddle of murky water can be seen the remains of what used to be an easy chair, the springs dangling helplessly, and the stuffing, soaked from two weeks' dampness, now sprouting tufts of grass—mute evidence of the indifference pervading the lives of the block's inhabitants. And yet, these people are an animated group, a restless army, always searching, always on the move. Their searching and their moving, symbols of their frustrations, manifest themselves in violent ways. It is when the dark hours come that these people begin to prowl.

Several of our workers were leaving one of our buildings one night, and as they started down the outside steps they saw a man lying there, blood flowing from a knife wound he had just sustained. We had a female cook who was beaten and robbed as she was leaving the Center one evening. As I was walking into a nearby restaurant one night, a man was being carried out on a stretcher. He was a pusher who had been shot to death by a drug addict. Women roam the block during the wee hours of the morning, trying to lure men from our buildings with promises of drugs and love.

More than anything, though, it is the noise that makes living on Clinton Avenue so difficult. It's more than the wail of police sirens, the roar of the fire engines, the screech of angry tires: it's the incessant screaming of people who are taking out their fury on one another, the howling of hordes of youngsters as they spill out onto the streets in quest of something to do, the raucous laughter and language of adults whose parties are ended only by exhaustion.

One night, the sound of guns crackled through the air. We didn't think much about it until one of our workers told us that one of the bullets had landed in his apartment. Tracing the path of the bullet from the marks it had left, he found that it had entered his apartment by crashing through the window next to his baby's crib, had ricocheted off a mirror and then had fallen harmlessly to the floor. Cindy was terrified. For the next few days she made sure that she ducked safely beneath any window that overlooked the street.

ten /...
···/ making every hour count

EXCEPT FOR A FEW who are committed into our care by the courts, the men in our program are there on their own. This means that they can walk out on us at any time. There are, naturally, several reasons why they don't all dash pell-mell for the door when temptation calls: they want to be free of drugs or whatever else is weighing them down; they have a certain amount of trust in us; they have a fear of the outside world; and they realize that as long as they remain with us they have a chance to overcome their problems, become a part of the Teen Challenge family, and, eventually, return to the outside world *without* fear.

There is always a member of our staff on duty at the downstairs desk at 416. The man on the morning shift comes in at 8:30 A.M. and is relieved by someone else at 2:30 in the afternoon, unless he himself remains on duty for a second shift, which ends at 9 P.M. Another person handles the desk from 9 until 1 in the morning, when he is replaced by a man who works the night watch, finishing up his tour of duty by awakening the men at 7:30.

Our purpose in having someone at the desk twenty-four hours a day is not just to answer the phone; that is only a small part of the job. Among the most important duties for the desk man are tending to the sick and counseling with the men. Sometimes one of the men will need emergency medical care, and it is the responsibility of the desk man to see to it that the man has a way of getting to the hospital. Counseling is a multifaceted job. Most of the men in our program have

100

dozens of questions about all sorts of things ranging from how they can get permission to go home to visit a sick grandmother to how to interpret a portion of the Bible. Counseling also involves trying to comfort those persons going through cold turkey and those who are afraid, lonely, depressed, worried or just plain unable to get to sleep.

Furthermore, the desk man serves as a receptionist and as a guard. He must intercept anyone who may be trying to leave the Center and he must attempt to talk him into not giving up so easily. He also is on the lookout for those who might be trying to circumvent our rules, especially those who have a desire to steal or those who are trying to sneak in a smoke. Several times each year our desk men, almost all of whom are reformed narcotics users, catch men who have been smoking marijuana at 416. Marijuana is brought in by visitors who are certain that they can get away with providing a smoke for one of our men. Those who have a few puffs take every precaution to avoid being caught: they rinse their mouths out with mouthwash, they brush their teeth, they wash their hands and faces, they douse themselves with cologne. It always amazes them when the desk man, who is familiar with the odor of marijuana and can usually sniff it a long way off, puts the pinch on them. Unlike the person who is caught smoking a cigarette, the man who has used marijuana is expelled from the Center the first time he is proved guilty.

We have learned that one of the most important factors in our rehabilitation program is to keep everyone busy: active, stimulated minds are less likely to be victimized by temptation. After much trial and error, we have settled down to a schedule that is busy enough to keep the men occupied and stimulating enough to make them look forward to each new day.

After the men have been awakened in the morning, have taken care of their work assignments and have finished breakfast, they are permitted to return to their rooms. At 10:30 each morning, Monday through Saturday, they must all attend services in our chapel at 444. Our devotions are conducted in both English and Spanish and consist of a message presented by one of our staff members, singing (the wife of one of our workers plays the organ at all our services), and prayer. When the service is over, which is usually about noon, everyone files into the cafeteria for lunch. Several of our female workers serve the food; when the meal is over, the men who are assigned to kitchen detail take care of washing the dishes, cleaning off the tables and sweeping the floors.

There are a number of similarities in the schedule for each day, yet no two days are exactly alike. Here is a day-by-day breakdown of the afternoon and evening activities during a typical week at Teen Challenge:

MONDAY

1:30-3:30—This time is spent in giving all the rooms at 416 a thorough going over and cleaning up.

3:30-4:30—Separate classes are conducted in Spanish and English, with staffers instructing the men in the fundamentals of the Christian faith. Classes are also divided into those for newcomers to our program and those for men who have graduated to advanced status. We take the men through the ABC's of Christian living, teaching them what sin is, how it originated, and how they can gain victory over it. Among the many other topics covered are instructions in how they can grow in Christian faith, what the Bible says about how a man is to conduct his life and what they can look forward to in a Christ-centered life.

In order to gain promotion to the advanced class, each student must pass an examination. Tests vary, but among the more standard questions a student must correctly answer are the following:

What is sin?
What must one do to be saved?
Name the 27 books of the New Testament and the 39 books of the Old Testament.
Quote these verses of Scripture: I John 1:9, Hebrews 9:27, Micah 6:18, Ephesians 2:8 and 9, Galatians 6:17, Romans 3:23, Jeremiah 29:13, II Timothy 2:15, Romans 6:6 and John 3:16.

Before anyone can graduate from the advanced class to begin the second phase of his rehabilitation at our farm in

Pennsylvania, where he will undergo further schooling or will be taught a trade, he must pass another examination. This test usually consists of questions such as these:

Quote the Ten Commandments.
Quote I John 4:8, Genesis 3:6, I Peter 2:21, Matthew 5:48, I Corinthians 10:13, I John 1:7, John 12:46, Romans 8:3, Matthew 22:36 through 40, Psalms 19:1 and Romans 1:20.
Define moral law, moral government, holiness, love.
What is meant by the term "self-denial" in Matthew 16:24?
What does it mean to "walk in the light"?
List three rewards of conformity to God's reasonable requirements.
List three consequences of non-conformity to God's reasonable requirements.

4:45-5:15—Prayertime.
5:30-6:30—Dinner hour. (This remains the same throughout the week.)
7:15-8:15—Another hour of classes similar to those held in the morning.
8:15————Monday evening is, for the most part, a night off. Many of the men take care of their laundry, do a little cleaning up in the dormitory or settle down for some talks with our staff counselors or for some group bull sessions.
Bedtime each evening is 11 P.M., by which time all lights in the upstairs rooms must be out and all the men must be bedded down.

TUESDAY

1:30-3:15—This time is set aside for work that must be done in our buildings and around the grounds. During the summer, the small lawn in front of our main building at 444 must be mowed. Other assignments given to the men include mopping floors, dusting, and washing windows.
3:30-4:30—Back to the classrooms.
4:45-5:15—Prayer.
7:15-8:00—Classes are not held on this evening, but the men are urged to use this time for studying.
8:00————Chapel services: a message by either a visiting

minister, one of our staffers or by me; group singing and praying.

WEDNESDAY

1:30-2:00—Prayer.

2:00-3:00—Classes.

3:15-5:00—Gym. The pastor of the Central Methodist Church, which is a few blocks from the Center, has graciously allowed us to use the large gymnasium in his building so that our men might have an opportunity to participate in some wholesome exercise.

7:15-8:15—Classes.

8:30———Hymn singing in our chapel. Occasionally we have a guest vocalist or instrumentalist. Usually, though, our none-too-talented vocalists merely engage in some loud singing, and I do mean *loud*.

THURSDAY

12:30-3:15—Everyone has to pitch in and help with the odd jobs around the Center. We cannot afford to have hired men come in and take care of such things as washing our trucks, fixing flat tires or polishing floors; even if we could afford it, we wouldn't change our present system, for we have found work to be one of the most beneficial phases of our life at Teen Challenge. It helps the men to learn how to take pride in doing a job well and teaches them the responsibility of not letting these tasks slip by and pile up.

3:30-4:30—Classes.

4:45-5:15—Time for prayer. If it seems that we spend a lot of time praying, the impression is correct. There is no substitute for prayer in the life of a Christian and there is no such thing as praying too much. These are precious and invaluable times for our patients, who soon learn that they can unburden their hearts to God in prayer, oftentimes saying things to Him that they would be afraid to tell to anyone else. There are many other benefits: the sense of well-being and peace that comes from having communed with the Lord, and

Inward cleansing is always manifested by a
desire to clean up the Center's facilities.

the answers to prayers that men who love Him sincerely come to expect.

7:15-8:15—Classes.

8:30————Visual aids. We try to have the men view the best of Christian movies and filmstrips. After the show we divide the men into two groups, fire questions at them about what they have just seen and answer any of their questions.

FRIDAY

2:00-3:30—Gym at a nearby Bedford Y.M.C.A. All the men are driven there in our nine-passenger vans. We tell the men that it is not mandatory that they take part in these physical exercise routines at the Y.M.C.A. or in the ones at the local church, but that if they do not join in they must stay at the Center and work. Rare is the man who chooses to mop a floor rather than play a little basketball or volleyball.

3:45-4:30—Classes, many of which throughout the week evolve into discussion periods. New Christians are encouraged to ask any and all questions they might have.

4:45-5:15—Prayer.

7:15-8:15—Classes.

8:30————Each Friday evening we endeavor to have a feature-length Christian film.

Time is also set aside on Friday for counseling sessions with Reverend Lester Eisenberger from Yonkers, New York. He ranges far and wide in his work at Teen Challenge, counseling with members of our staff as well as with men and women who are going through our treatment program. We have long been aware that some of the people who come to us have deep-seated problems that need tender care and, more than that, care from someone who has an understanding of mental and emotional illnesses. Some of the boys at the Center make special requests to see Reverend Eisenberger. There are some problems that these men prefer not to mention to our staff members, and we respect this. Reverend Eisenberger has been of invaluable service in getting through to many of the ones who have serious disturbances, in getting through to those who merely want to unburden themselves, and in getting through to our workers. The result has been that the addicts have come to have a better understanding of themselves and their problems, we have been able to gain a better comprehension of their strengths and weaknesses, and our staff has come to know one another more intimately.

SATURDAY

1:00-4:30—Visitors are allowed. This is often an emotional period for our men, some of whom are seeing their loved ones for the first time in weeks or months or even years. It is also an afternoon of unique significance for the parents, wives, children, brothers, sisters and friends of our patients. These outsiders have no idea what to expect. All they know is that their loved one was a drug addict, has been ill or has been a delinquent. They want to believe that their loved ones are well or at least on the way to recovery, but so many of these people have been deceived before that they are afraid to raise their hopes too high. After the preliminary round of handshakes, hugs, kisses and tears, everyone steps back to look each other over.

Saturday afternoons are also the time for the patients to take care of any personal business that has to be tended to. If such is the case, we have one of our staff members take the person wherever he must go and then escort him back to the Center.

4:30————Prayer.

7:30————Family Rally. This is a chapel service that is open to the public.

SUNDAY

The men are taken to various churches to attend services in the morning and evening, but aside from that and a 4:30 afternoon prayer get-together, they have the day to themselves.

For several years, the start of each new day at Teen Challenge was signalled at 7:30 A.M. by the ringing of a cowbell by the person who was on night duty at 416. This may sound like a rather crude substitute for an alarm clock, but it served its purpose. In fact, the bell not only was rung to awaken people in the morning, it was also sounded to let them know it was time to come to chapel and to gather for our evening snack. It may have been an inelegant way of rounding everyone up, but it was an effective one.

As quaint as the old cowbell was in its own way, it has passed out of use. Today, we use a loudspeaker system that is connected to every room in 416. The means of awakening the addicts are as varied as the personalities of the men on night duty. One fellow will wake up everyone ever so gently at 7:30 A.M. by playing some soft music over the intercom system. Another will loudly announce that it's time to get out of bed. Some softly read portions of Scripture. One man used to start singing at 7:30 A.M. There wasn't anybody who could sleep through *his* singing; he was loud and awful and his baritone voice droned on and on in a monotone that drove people out of bed to escape it.

For the sleepy bodies who managed to snore through everything, there was one sure means of rousing them: someone would roll them right out of bed and onto the floor. Because the men are hungry for breakfast, it has never been too much of a problem getting them up in the morning, though. A bigger problem has been in dealing with those who are too lazy to make their beds and tidy up their rooms before coming to chow. We used to keep after these lazy ones, but they often got away with their sloppiness because it was so hard to keep up with all the other work we had to take care of. One day at our staff meeting of workers we hashed out the situation. Several of our counselors asked me what they should do. I said, "What does the Bible say? The Apostle Paul said that if a man doesn't work he isn't entitled to eat. I think what you should do is to check all the beds in the morning and if you find some of them unmade you should not allow those men to eat. Just call down to 444 and give someone a list of the men who didn't make their beds. And tell the man at 444 to call all those offenders out of the breakfast line and send them back to make their beds. To really make this sort of thing work, you'll have to show them that you mean business and to do this you'll have to make those men remain in their rooms and miss breakfast."

The new idea was put to the test the next morning and the men who were called back to make their beds went along with the whole thing without a grumble—until they learned that their laziness was going to cost them a chance to go back and fill their bellies. There was an immediate increase in bedmaking and since that time we have had little trouble in getting the men to tidy up. The lessons learned by the stomach are quickly passed along to the mind and muscles.

This upsurge in taking care of household duties is not so much prompted by a desire for cleanliness as it is by a desire for food. As long as a person is on drugs, he usually has little interest in food. The combination of not eating properly and feasting on narcotics wracks a person's body and makes most addicts look like walking corpses—hollow-eyed, sallow of complexion, gaunt. Once they have gone through cold turkey, they want to make up for all the meals they have missed. Suddenly, their systems come alive, their bodies long for the food they have so long been without. It is exciting to see life spring back into their bodies, to see them take on a healthy appearance, to watch as they turn from their stoop-shouldered way of walking or standing and take an upright stance.

Addicts who are coming off drugs normally "chock," which is a term they use to mean that they are putting on a lot of weight. They have tremendous desires for certain foods, especially for sweets and starches. We are not always able to oblige the men by offering them seconds, but when the cook does yell out "Seconds," the scene in the cafeteria is a cherished sight. No sooner has the magic word been shouted than there is a frantic clattering of chairs and a pounding of feet across the floor as the men rush to the food counter, their plates outstretched.

In chapel we continually remind the men that all of our food has been provided by the goodness of others, either in the form of direct contributions of foodstuffs or in the form of money that has enabled us to make our purchases. It has always brought warm and wonderful thoughts to me to ponder the kindnesses that have made Teen Challenge possible. Not a day goes by that we at the Center don't offer prayers of thanks for all that has come our way.

Most of our food pickups are made by a young man named Randy, who climbs aboard our nine-passenger sports van and makes numerous trips to markets and warehouses. Each month he makes a trip to the U.S. government warehouse in The Bronx, where he obtains such things as powdered milk, flour, butter, peanut butter, jam and jelly. The amounts we are given vary from month to month, but our 100 pounds of rice is a ration that we can pretty well count on at all times.

It has been our policy never to beg. Doors have been opened to us simply because of who we are and what the Lord has undertaken for us. When Randy asks at the market for seventy or eighty pork chops, the butcher does a double take; his first question is usually something like, "Good grief, how many kids do you have in your family?" When the butcher finds out where Randy is from, he usually gives him a discount.

Even more of a problem than getting food has been that of trying to find a cook to prepare our meals. When we have a full house (this includes addicts, workers and the children of the workers) we have close to seventy-five people who have to be fed three times a day. Recently we were fortunate to have found a man named Dominic to serve as our permanent chef. Dominic has been a professional cook for years, and now that he has joined us we are eating better than ever. Our past has not always been filled with such sumptuous feasts.

Being a cook at Teen Challenge is not an easy job, as we have been well aware. There have been an ample number of reasons why it has been impossible for us to keep a person on the job for any length of time. Our wage scale is certain not to attract a master chef, and another drawback was the small size of the kitchen when we had it in 416. Not the least of the problems was to try to satisfy the appetites of men from the many nationalities represented at Teen Challenge. We have never expected our cooks to serve up special dishes to suit the tastes of all our people every day, but we have tried to see to it that there was a good variety that would be pleasing, palatable and nourishing to all. Long ago we became aware that if we satisfied the demands of a man's stomach we were meeting one of his most vital needs, creating in him a sense of well-being and demonstrating to him that we were going to keep our promise of taking care of his every need.

Until Dominic came along we had had a succession of cooks who seemed to be blown in the front door by one breeze and out the back door by another. We prayed about the situation, but, try as we might, we were never able to retain anyone in our kitchen for more than six months. We have used men from our own program as cooks and we have had others who have come to us from as far away as Alabama and Texas. Nobody, however, made quite as lasting an impression as did Monday, a Southerner with an ability to turn the simplest meal into a case of roaring indigestion. Worse yet, Monday was the sort of person who left a bad taste in one's mouth in several ways.

Monday was what I would call a spiritual con man. He had worked in dozens of missions from Maine to Oregon and he had learned all of the tricks along the route. His personality was as pliable as Silly Putty. Monday could burst forth in prayer and sound like a preacher with a handful of degrees. He was equally fluent in the language of the streets and every now and then would show us this purple portion of his vocabulary. I was always of the opinion that Monday was sort of an Elmer Gantry of the pantry.

When he came to work in the morning, his helpers in the kitchen would ask him what should be prepared for breakfast. Monday's reply was a standard, "I gets my menu from the Lord. He always tells me what to make." Then he would pause, roll his eyes heavenward, and drop into a moment of deep meditation as he awaited his orders. When he felt that he had been given his instructions, Monday would slowly turn to his helpers and pronounce his breakfast menu, invariably saying, "This mo'nin' the Lord say we is gonna have corn flakes."

Monday liked nothing better than to brag about the quality of his meals. He seemed to believe that merely because there had been no increase in the mortality rate and because we kept coming back to the cafeteria day after day that we were admirers of his greasy cooking. He used to go from table to table trying to get compliments. I didn't have the heart to tell Monday my feelings, but one day I leaned over to the man sitting next to me and told him, "I think this meal was prepared by the devil and not the Lord. It tastes more like Satan's Supper than the Lord's Lunch."

One of our workers finally came to me and said, "Brother Don, you've got to get a legitimate cook. I can't take any more of Monday. I've taken all my salary for the past few weeks to go out and buy food so that my wife and I could have a decent meal now and then."

I would have complied with this request if I had been able to find someone—anyone—who could have made so much as a slice of toast. Finally, we got a replacement for Monday. I suppose that we saved some money on food during Monday's reign because no one wanted seconds, but by the time we got rid of him the people at the Center looked like a flock of hummingbirds on a Weight Watchers' diet.

eleven /...
···/ who are these people?

THE RESULTS OF OUR PROGRAM have been so fruitful that we have run into a new and unexpected problem recently: we no longer have adequate space to take care of all who come to us seeking admittance. In a way, I suppose that I should be grateful that we have reached such a position. Nevertheless, it grieves me to have to turn away needy people. Ideally, we would throw open the doors and welcome in every one of those persons who earnestly seeks to find a new starting point in life.

As our work has become more widely known and respected, instead of having to seek candidates for our program a waiting list of about twenty-five men has become standard. As a result, we have had to abandon part of our street-corner ministry and concentrate our efforts on caring for those needy ones who come to us from all directions, some of their own accord, having heard or read about Teen Challenge, and others sent to us by ministers or interested laymen, both in our own community and from around the nation. Large numbers of cases are referred to us by the courts.

We have always been careful about who we admit, but because of the number of applications we are currently receiving we have made our screening process doubly tough. This is especially true in the case of those referred to us by the courts. We are pleased that the penal authorities think enough of us to send people to us for help, yet we have to be certain that those who are sent our way are truly desirous of committing themselves to our care.

Who are these people who come to us for help? They are

113

dope users, prostitutes, thieves; they are schizophrenics, homo-sexuals, alcoholics; they are gang leaders, manic-depressives, un-wanted children. They walk the streets by night, grovel in alleyways and stench-filled rooms by day. Life holds little meaning for them. They live in the present so that they can forget their past. For them there is no future, only a bewilder-ing *now*. There is no way of making a composite of a typical person at Teen Challenge. Each is an individual in need of care that will suit his particular malady.

I asked one sixteen-year-old with effeminate features if he was a boy or a girl and he replied in a high-pitched voice, "I don't know."

When we told one boy that we would like to contact his parents to let them know where he was, he shrugged his should-ers and told us, "Don't bother. We got fifteen kids in the family. They won't even miss me at home."

Some of the older men get a rather sheepish look when we question them about their marital status. The reply usually runs along these lines: "I'm not exactly married, but I got nine kids," followed by a recital of the details—how they were mar-ried once, ran off with another girl, then with yet another, and how they have lost track of their original wife, whom they assume is no longer their responsibility. Restructuring family life for such men is a job filled with legal complexities and emotional U-turns.

A young man who came to us from New England told us honestly of his mental problems—that he suffered from periods of excruciating depression and that he had tried to commit suicide. When he arrived at the Center, he brought with him enough bottles of pills to have stocked a drug store: tranquil-izers to settle him down, stimulants to get him going, as well as a collection of others to take care of his every need. The first time he reached for one of those bottles, we said to him, "Unh-unh. Around here, our only medicine is a liberal dose of God's word to be taken as often as needed."

It was as hard for him to give up those pills as it was for addicts to give up their drugs. Somewhat reluctantly, he con-sented to push aside his bottles and stay with us, giving up an excellent job in order to remain with us long enough to be helped. It was not an easy decision for him, but he explained his willingness to remain at the Center by saying, "My life is more important than any job."

Another man, in his early 30's, sent to us by a pastor in Kansas City, was a truck driver who had become accustomed to taking large doses of pep pills to keep himself awake for long stretches of time when he was making lengthy trips. As so often happens, the pep pills led to other things, and before long he was hooked on drugs. He lost his job and his wife and was simply wasting away. Before this man came to us, his pastor phoned to ask if we would accept him at the Center. I told him that we would, but as a test of the man's sincerity I asked the pastor to have him come to his church for a week. If he was able to fulfill this obligation, then we would begin to believe that he really was seeking help.

A week later we met the man at the airport. He was in such bad shape that we practically had to carry him to the car. While on the plane, he had given himself a shot of dope, which led me to think that his quest for a cure might not have been as sincere as I had been hoping. As had happened with several others, though, he fooled me, and it was a pleasure to watch him progress at the Center. He now has a good job as an automobile mechanic for a Christian who is a car dealer in Ohio.

An unusual case was that of Johnny, a narcotics addict from a wealthy family. When he tried to explain his problem to his parents, they would not believe that he was taking "goof balls," drinking cough syrup and shooting up with heroin. They preferred to think that he had been making all this up. They finally realized the severity of their son's condition when he pleaded with them to be sent to a hospital for treatment; this course of action, however, would have been a blight on their social record, so they called Teen Challenge.

Although it took courage for Johnny's parents to admit that their son was an addict, they tried to pass it off as an almost trivial difficulty that could be taken care of in a matter of days. These people insisted upon keeping one eye on their social standing and only one on their son. Had they kept both eyes on Johnny, he would never have fallen victim to dope.

Someone has defined the upper crust as "a bunch of crumbs

held together by a little dough." That is a rather narrow-minded view, but it is true that more and more members of the middle and upper classes are relying on drugs, possibly because they are far better able to come up with the money for them than are the members of the lower economic classes. College campuses also have become infested with heroin, marijuana and LSD. This is a distressing commentary on our times, but indicative of these troubled days in which men of all creeds, skin colorations and financial standings are so dissatisfied with life that they seek solace even in those things which they know will destroy them.

One Sunday evening, after speaking at a large church in a well-to-do community in northern New Jersey, the pastor said to me, "Don't let the affluence of this town fool you. We may not have the same kind of ghetto life that you are familiar with in New York, but behind the walls of these lavish homes here you will find the ghetto of the heart. Our young people may not be addicts, but they are empty and unsatisfied."

Through our doors have come the rich and the poor, the pimps and the pushers, the sick and the lonely. From time to time, I just sit and think about those who have come and gone. One of the men I like to recall is Benny. He had been caught in a narcotics crackdown in Yonkers, New York, several years ago and had come to know the Lord at Teen Challenge. This did not impress the judge, who sentenced him to two years in prison. When Benny went to jail he left his wife and five children behind. A large drug ring was operating within the prison and some of his fellow inmates threatened him with bodily harm because of his Christian stand and his unwillingness to partake in the corruption and vice that was so much a part of prison life. After a brawl in the jail, in which he was not actually a participant, Benny was given ten days in solitary confinement. When his ten days were up, he was brought before the warden. Benny apologized to the warden for what had happened and the warden, who had by then received reports that had cleared Benny of any part in the brawl, couldn't quite get over that.

Not long after this, I received a letter from Benny which read:

"I want to say at this time that my faith in the Lord grows stronger each day. I have been able to talk to some of the men here and a few are interested in being helped, and I hope to be able to send some down to Teen Challenge for further help in accepting and serving the Lord. When I left Teen Challenge, I never thought I would be doing what I am trying to do for these men. I give thanks to the Lord for what He has done for me and also for the help you and everyone else at Teen Challenge gave to me while I was there. I have come to find out that there is never enough time when you are serving the Lord. Reverend Don, I want to ask for prayer for my wife Tina and for my children.—The Lord's Humble Servant, BENNY"

Letters from these people are revealing, so let's take a look at a few more of them. The first is a condensation of a six-page letter sent to us by a teenage girl.

"I come from a very good home and my parents love me very much. I am active in school, church, and in helping others. I am on the yearbook staff, vice-president of my class, leader in an achievement group, leader in our church youth group, and a member of important clubs and activity groups. I visit in hospitals, I'm active in church, in many school projects, and am always trying to help others. I am considered popular in school, teachers say I have a good future, my parents think of me as a model child, the pastor and the church all think I am kind, considerate, and good. I smile, am personable, and to look at my picture you would never know what I am really like!

"I am a big phony. This is all a big front. Behind the smile is a confused, broken heart. I have thought of suicide twice. I steal ball-point pens from the five and dime store. I am not what people think I am. I really don't know God, and I am almost like a robot that goes through all the actions. I am not honest."

Next is a portion from the testimony of a former hippie named Bob Israel:

"I was born into a well-to-do family in Long Island, New York. My father is a doctor. At eight years of age I started stealing money from my mother's pocketbook to buy stamps for my stamp collection. I received quite a substantial allowance and yet I would also steal from my father's wallet. I vainly vowed that I would put it back as secretly as it was taken.

"A classmate offered me my first marijuana cigarette when I was 15. I smoked marijuana for a couple of years without my parents knowing. They were too busy socializing. I was a good student, but started to hang with the beats and the pill users. In my junior year in high school I started taking barbiturates, Benzedrene, and tranquilizers, along with marijuana. I let my hair grow and must have been one of the first hippie-type people in the Long Island area.

"My parents finally found out that I was smoking pot. I lied about where I got it. They decided to send me to a private school in Massachusetts. I still managed to get pot and pills there and to get drunk also. I became interested in Zen Buddhism and Yoga.

"When I graduated, I decided to leave home. I took money out of the bank and went to the Haight-Ashbury section of San Francisco. There I lived with my hippie friends. I tried LSD only once, but it left me more confused. My hair was now down to my shoulders and my Zen diet left me very skinny, so I must have looked like an old man.

"I spent much time reading poetry. One poem called *Jerusalem* had a line reading, 'Take up thy Cross, Oh Israel, and follow Jesus.' Because my name is Israel, I associated myself with it and began carving crosses.

"Several months later, an old lady invited me to a mission. Three days later I came and sat on a bench with several alcoholics and heard the word of God. At the end of the sermon I walked up with several others and the woman came and prayed with me. They gave me the address of a church called Glad Tidings. They, in turn, referred me to Teen Challenge, San Francisco. There I saw drug addicts—real heroin addicts— completely cured and cleansed by the power of God. It was here that I saw the power of prayer demonstrated and heard what Jesus Christ could do for lost humanity. I recognized my need of a Saviour and gave my heart and life to the Lord on February 18, 1967."

Bunny was a man who was not as affluent or as intellectual, perhaps, as Bob Israel, yet he struggled to find not only a decent way to live, but a reason to make life worth living. This is Bunny's story:

"When I had my first taste of heroin, I loved it. By the time I had reached 17, I was a nervous wreck, self-conscious and full of complexes. I was always depressed and life was hell on earth to me.

"After a while, the price of stuff went up and I got strung out. I stopped working and learned to steal. I would boost steaks: I could make it out of a super market with four or five nice sirloins under my belt. Sometimes I'd get busted and either go to jail or catch a beating from the manager. At first I hated to steal, but before long I couldn't pass a super market without a strong desire to go in and see what I could sneak out the door with. I didn't like hurting other people, but if it came to a choice between my getting high or someone getting hurt, well, it would be all right once I got high.

"Then I met the girl who is now my wife. Mary was also on junk. Our first night together, Mary wondered if two people who really loved each other could stop using drugs. For the first time in many years, I loved someone more than I loved satisfying my need for dope.

"We decided to go into Manhattan General Hospital, kick, and straighten up. We had both been to many hospitals before we met, but now we thought things would be different. We would come out clean and live together and for one another.

"After twenty-one days in Manhattan General, we went on welfare, got a small room and tried to make a new way of life for ourselves. Our plans didn't work. We had faith in each other and we loved each other, but we were still rotten inside. We began to argue. We began to get pleasure out of torturing each other. More often than not, Mary had a black eye. As long as we stayed off drugs, Mary was even more nervous than I was. There were times when I would make her so nervous that she would take fits and convulsions. We went back on drugs so we could calm down a little.

"One night while waiting for Mary on 96th Street and Broadway, I was scooped up for consenting to obtain narcotics. I was back in a cell in the Tombs, making it my fifteenth trip there. Usually when I would sit in my cell, I would say a prayer that went something like this: 'God, get me out of here and I'll never get in trouble again.' This time I felt moved to pray, but it was a different prayer. I thought, 'God, it seems like things are going from bad to worse, but for some reason, I feel that you have been doing something in my life and I'm leaving the future up to you.' For the first time in my life, I prayed expecting God to do something for me.

"A few days later, my case was thrown out and Mary and I had just smashed a store window so that we could get merchandise to sell and have enough money for heroin. While we were standing on 96th Street waiting for a connection to show up, I started to think about a drug addict friend of mine who had stopped fooling around with junk. He had told me about a church in The Bronx where he and many other boys had been freed from the drug habit.

"I reminded Mary about our friend and asked her if she would go with me to the church. She thought I suddenly had gone crazy. But Mary gave in and up we went. At the Damascus Church we met drug addicts who were staying clean. One of them took us in a corner and told us the power of God was keeping him clean. He told us a lot of other things, but we didn't understand. What we did understand was that he was clean. There was no room for us at Damascus, so they gave us the name of Teen Challenge.

"When we came to Teen Challenge, we were skinny and dirty. Little by little, we took our faith out of the things of this world and put our faith in Jesus Christ. He did nothing but reward us. Even before we knew our Lord as our own Saviour, He blessed us. He gave us a peace and calm right from the beginning and each day did a work in our lives.

"Mary is now so calm and happy that people who remember her past now gape when they see her. Christ has removed the dependent, clinging love we had for each other and replaced it with a real love for each other and for those around us and for Him. He has given us everything we have and now we try to give everything we have to His service."

To this Mary adds these closing comments:

"Salvation was very hard for me to accept in the beginning. I wanted to earn it, to do something for it. God did a miracle here, because I was raised on religion by nuns in Mother Cabrini's Convent, and as a result my heart was very hard towards the gospel. I knew all about Jesus, but I didn't know Jesus, as I do now, as my personal Savior and personal friend. What a difference. You can know all there is to know about someone without ever knowing him personally. As I sat under the gospel and the teaching of the Bible at Teen Challenge, though, something wonderful happened: my heart opened to the full knowledge that salvation was a free gift of God and that all I had to do was to accept it. I accepted it, and my joy has been unspeakable.

"Two weeks after entering Teen Challenge, Bunny and I were given a beautiful Christian wedding. Now we are studying to be missionaries. There are those who have never even heard of Jesus once. We want to tell them. Someone came and told us."

These are some of the people who come to us. In their own way, they each frantically searched for happiness and a purpose for living. Their quest brought them to a reliance upon Benzedrene, cough syrup, marijuana, money, Zen Buddhism, hippie living, involvement in school and church activities, promiscuous sex, heroin, physical love, and hospital cures. Not a single one of those remedies did any good. All of these people—men and women, rich and poor, Negro, Puerto Rican and white—found what they were looking for only when they turned to Jesus Christ.

twelve /...
···/ five projects to
/ pray about

A WOMAN'S SCREAMS cut razor-like through the late afternoon. I hurried out to the street, where a knot of people had already gathered around the woman, who by now was sobbing deeply. As I got closer, I saw that the woman was Cookie Rivera and that she was kneeling beside her five-year-old son Dondi, who lay limp and blood-stained in the middle of the road.

"Please, God, take care of him," Cookie began praying.

An eyewitness to what had taken place told me, "Dondi was running across the street. He ran right in front of this car. The driver says he didn't see him. He knew he had hit something, but he thought it was a dog. He must have dragged the poor kid under the car for fifty, sixty feet."

"Please, God, take care of him," Cookie kept praying.

God did take good care of Dondi, who spent the next few weeks limping around with a cast on his broken leg but who mended quickly and completely. The effects of that accident, however, were more far-reaching than that. For more than a year, Dave and I had discussed the need for a new home for the women in the program.

"This incident proves that we also need a home for the children," I said to Dave.

"I know, I know," he said. "It's not going to be easy finding places for the girls and the children and it won't be easy to raise the money. We've got to make these things a matter of urgent prayer."

We had already been praying about three other needs,

namely, for a place where we could send the men from the Center for further guidance and training, for a school where they could go for advanced Bible study, and for a re-entry program to prepare men to rejoin society. All these places were musts, for we now knew that our work had to be divided into two phases: evangelism and rehabilitation. One without the other was not sufficient. A person who stayed at the Center for several months and remained free of drugs for that length of time still had far to go before he could be considered cured. We had already set up a rehabilitation program on a Pennsylvania farm, but it was only in the beginning stages.

One of the joys of being a Christian is that we never have to hesitate about asking God to supply our needs as long as we know they are within His will. But were we overloading the Lord now by asking Him to take care of five such important situations? Faithful as always, the Lord took care of each of our requests one by one, proving again that nothing is impossible for Him.

Included in our prayers were added petitions for people who could run each of these places. This was particularly true in the case of the women. Earlier, we thought their problems had been solved when we had relocated them on a picturesque estate in Rhinebeck, New York. That project had to be abandoned after a year, however, because we lacked a director for it.

Our ministry among the girls had always floundered far behind the rest of our work. What few women we had in Brooklyn were housed in 405, which was across the street from our other buildings. It was an undesirable setup. Women succumbed more easily to the call of the outside world, were upset by the slightest thing that went wrong, and always had a harder time breaking their drug habit than did the men. Thus, it was imperative that we find a highly competent person to be their director.

The urgency of our needs was made dramatically clear by what happened to Danny and Bobbie. Danny became one of our most ardent converts after ridding himself of drugs and we thought so highly of him that we retained him at the Center as a counselor. He fell in love with Bobbie, one of the girl addicts undergoing treatment at the Center, a relationship that was detrimental to both. Trouble was on the horizon. We saw it coming, but were helpless to do much about it. In the double tragedy that soon followed, Danny stole a car and was shot by a policeman, and Bobbie, who by then had left Teen Challenge, took an overdose of drugs and died.

As so often has been the case, the way to climb up and out of our dilemma did not come until we had sunk as far down as we could go. Our first upward step had come when we were able to establish the Teen Challenge Training Center in Rehrersburg, Pennsylvania. To all of us it is known as "the farm." It is located in the Pennsylvania Dutch countryside, 160 acres of land just a three-hour, 130-mile drive from Clinton Avenue.

Reverend Frank Reynolds is in charge of our operations in Rehrersburg. He took an interest in Teen Challenge during its earliest days, at which time he was the pastor of a church on Staten Island. Almost from the very beginning, Reverend Reynolds urged us to establish a follow-up program for men who came to our Center, insisting that getting men off drugs or out of gang life would not be sufficient.

For some of the men it is two or three weeks before they can get a good night's sleep at the farm. All their lives they have been used to noise—the screeching of subways, the wail of fire and police sirens, the night screams that mingle with the incessant clatter and chatter of street life. One man came to breakfast at the farm one morning and complained, "I couldn't sleep a wink all night because of the noise."

"What noise?" someone asked.

"All those crickets."

Other men have a hard time sleeping because they are so excited about being out in the country. They act like little children, and they are full of questions about plants and animals they are seeing for the first time. It is a rare individual, however, who does not soon get caught up in the peace and serenity of this country living.

It is on the farm that we get the men to understand the meaning of hard-core Christian commitment and it is where we prepare them to step back into the world, a world that will be strangely different to them now that they have been saved.

They are told that they are on the honor system at the farm, far more than they had been at the Center. At the farm we stop telling them, "We cannot trust you." Instead, we say to them, "Your being here makes it evident that you have made some progress as a Christian and, as a result, we will trust you unless you do something that causes us to remove that trust."

We like to have a man remain at the farm for six months or longer so that we will have time to give him some Bible teaching that will go far beyond the mere memorization of verses. After a person has been in Rehrersburg for approximately two months, he is interviewed by a staff member to determine the direction in which he should aim his life. This is a thought that has seldom, if ever, crossed the minds of most of these men. They are told that we are ready, willing and able to teach them a trade or further their Christian education. Some men have pressing financial problems or have families to support and must forego schooling so that they can launch out immediately into the workaday world. There have been instances of men who felt compelled to get a job so that they could repay money to people they had stolen from.

For those who desire to be taught a trade, the Bible study workload is cut down so that more time can be spent in one of our vocational training programs. We have facilities for training cooks, carpenters, printers, automobile mechanics and farmers. Skilled instructors work with the pupils so that they will be proficient enough to qualify for a job in their chosen field by the time they leave the farm. We found out early that those who were unable to get employment often drifted back into the same trouble that had brought them to Teen Challenge in the first place.

The final phase of our rehabilitation—a re-entry program— has also been set up. It involves giving final instructions and guidance for those who are ready to return to their neighborhood. Going home is often a terror-filled experience. For some, it is the problem of how to adjust to family life; for others it is a matter of how to maintain their Christian witness in a way that will attract other people rather than repel them. We house these men at 405, thus enabling them to retain a link with Teen Challenge while they rejoin society and start a new job.

Now that they are ready to take up their places in the everyday world, we emphasize to them the importance of being more than ordinary 9-to-5 working men. Holding a steady job is a real accomplishment for these men, but, we tell them, letting them know the obligation they have to help their fellow men, God wants them not to be afraid of Christian involvement. Some of them feel that because they are not ministers or full-time Christian workers, they can please God if they spend a few minutes each day in reading the Bible and another minute here or there in quick snatches of prayer. Christian commitment, we remind them, goes far beyond this and there is for each person a job that God has set aside to be done.

One of the most unexpected causes for concern was church attendance. It was not that they didn't want to go; quite the contrary, many of these men complained that they were unable to go to church often enough. This situation was an outcropping from the supersaturation of churchlife that we gave them at the Center and the farm. At both places they went to chapel services morning and night six days a week and to outside churches twice on Sundays. In addition, they frequently attended other religious services with outside groups and took part in daily prayer groups, study sessions, and discussions. Only when these men had been thrust back into their neighborhoods did they realize they had been living busy-as-a-bee Christian lives. Things were different there; they attended church on Sunday, but found that the activity was often stagnant compared to ours. Now, long before they leave us, we begin indoctrinating them about this situation so that they will be able to get used to attending two or three services a week instead of two or three a day.

Having a farm and a re-entry program took care of two of our five major requests. A third answer to our prayers materialized when we purchased a home in suburban Long Island, where we could house children and where we could set up a foster-care program for placement of such youngsters. Although this is the smallest of our ministries so far as the number of participants is concerned, it has been and always will be entitled to a special place in the hearts of all of us. For years we were unable to give much assistance to the children of the parents who came to us to be cured. If one of the parents was with us, it meant that the other one had to work and that in turn created the problem of caring for the child or children in the family. If both parents were at the Center, the situation was bad, although sometimes not so bad as if just the father or the mother were absent. When both parents were undergoing care, relatives usually took charge of the children. Where only the one parent was being treated, the compassion and understanding of other people was not aroused as readily; people assumed that the one parent would be able to take care of the family and a job. More often than not this was a false belief.

Far worse than the indifference of outsiders was the indifference of the parents. Children, many of them babies, were sometimes left untended for days at a stretch—some left in their cribs, others strapped into high chairs—while their parents went on an alcoholic or drug binge. Hundreds of youngsters were suffering from malnutrition and thousands of others from the lack of love, forerunners of serious illnesses that were sure to ravage them in later years.

The opening of our home for children and the establishment of our foster-care program on Long Island fulfilled a vision that had been with us for years. Although most of the children we take care of are those of parents who are under treatment at the Center, we also take in others. Ours will soon be recognized as a State-approved children's home. This will help us in many ways and enable us to take in court-appointed children.

What makes this work so disheartening at times is that a mother sometimes wants her child back. These children are not ours, so we must relinquish them when a parent makes such a request. If we feel certain that the parent sincerely wants the child back and is motivated by love, then we don't mind giving up the child. All too often, though, a parent wants the child back only so that he or she will be able to claim additional welfare benefits.

Gloom has never prevailed for long in any of our ministries and in the case of the children, the moments of frustration have been heavily outnumbered by the hours of reward. Unless the children of drug users get help, the odds are skyhigh against their living happy, normal, drug-free lives.

One thing the Lord kept showing us was that as long as we had the faith to step out boldly He had the means to uphold us. This is exactly what enabled us to found the Teen Challenge Institute of Missions, a Bible school in Rhinebeck, New York. There would not be any such school, though, had it not been for the kindness of the man who has been motivated so often by the Lord to come to our rescue in moments of need— W. Clement Stone. When he heard of our plans for the school and of our lack of funds, Stone bought the estate in Rhinebeck for $175,000 and then let us use it to establish the school. Our enrollment may be small, but I doubt that there is a school anywhere with a lovelier campus. It is nestled in an area of unique beauty: soft, rolling hills and stately trees provide a pervading peacefulness that engulfs those who draw near to it. The estate once belonged to the Astors. There are 100 acres of land on which stands a 30-room mansion built of native stone in 1928 for the late Alice Astor, wife of Colonel Serge Oblensky, the Russian who renounced his title after World War I in order to become an American citizen.

Our school was founded so that graduates from the Teen Challenge program could obtain advanced Christian education. Large numbers of these people had difficulty gaining admission to Bible schools because they had done so poorly in grade school and high school. The Teen Challenge Institute of Missions is conducted on a trimester basis of three four-month terms each year. It is a two-year school. In the spring of 1968 we had twenty-nine students, some of whom, like others before them, will go on to other schools after graduating from ours. Another seventeen men and eight women from our Center attended other schools. Most of these were Spanish-speaking people who had to go to schools where their native tongue was spoken.

Setting up a school was something that we at Teen Challenge were not familiar with, and the process of lining up a staff and formulating a curriculum were worrisome items that set all of us to scratching our heads. (John Kenzy, who had worked with us for several summers, did a fine job of getting things organized.) There was no single dilemma that caused more scratching than our quest for a man to run the school. We looked near and far for a headmaster, but it was not until we looked as far away as Rhodesia that we found our man, Reverend Edmund Cooksey. Someone had advised us that Reverend Cooksey was highly qualified and, in light of the trouble that was cropping up in Rhodesia at the time, that he might be interested in a position such as the one we had to offer. For a brief time we debated whether we could afford the expense of bringing him all the way from Rhodesia. It was a short debate: we soon knew enough about Reverend Cooksey, an Englishman who had taught in Long Island as well as in Rhodesia, to convince us that he was our man.

With four of our five specific prayer requests answered, we watched to see how God would fulfill the last and most difficult one. With as many as three dozen men living at the Center, it was all I could do to make certain that their program functioned smoothly. Only spare moments were devoted to the women's program. Female staffers such as Hope, Elishea, Sharon, and dozens of others did the best they could, as did an occasional male who felt that he might be of assistance. Even so, for the most part it was to little avail. We continued praying for a new home for the girls and for a person who would be a suitable leader for the project.

Working in reverse order—at least that is the way it seemed to us at the time—the Lord first provided the man we needed. While Dave was in Seattle, Washington, he met John Benton, a Youth for Christ director. Their first encounter was at the airport where John asked Dave, "May I help you carry your luggage?" Since that day, John Benton has been helping to carry much of the workload for Teen Challenge. He arrived in 1965, and it was soon apparent that this gentleman with a round face and a quick smile had a capacity for doing much work and for doing it well.

One of John's first projects was to find a new home for our girls. Together with his wife Elsie, he looked for months, scouring places as far as 150 miles from the Center. I went with the Bentons on one of their scouting missions to Garrison, New York, which is some 40 miles south of Rhinebeck. As we drove away from a property that the realtor had just been showing to us, I saw an area with a large open field and a big stone house set in the background. This estate was situated along the Hudson River directly across the water from the West Point Military Academy. It was an idyllic setting. Out loud I said, "Now there's the kind of place we're looking for."

My enthusiasm was quickly muzzled by the realtor, who told us, "The asking price for that property would be between $225,000 and $275,000—if it were available, which it is not." I could feel myself slowly sinking. Why did I have to have such a rich taste? Why did I have to take an interest in an area where the Roosevelts, Vanderbilts and Astors had maintained estates?

Several weeks later, John said to me, "I got a call today from the realtor and he says he has a place for us to look at."

"Where is it?" I asked.

An ample grin spread across John's face where it lingered for a long time before he said, "It's in Garrison, right across the road from the other place we looked at up there. Remember it?"

"Do I remember? How could I forget?"

John and Elsie looked at the property, and when John returned to the office he was ecstatic, floating on Cloud 9, as he described the estate.

"What are they asking for it?" I said to John.

"It's like a dream up there," said John, oblivious to my question.

"John, how much does it cost?"

"There are huge flowerbeds filled with . . ."

"How much, John?" I asked, raising my voice slightly. "How much?"

John had known that he could put me off only so long. It was sad to watch him descend, comparatively speaking, into a fog bank as he lowered his voice and muttered, "Two hundred and sixty-five thousand dollars."

"Go get it," I told him.

As I left John's office, I knew he was in a state of semishock. This was going to be his first chance to do the impossible, for we were entrusting him with full responsibility for the girls' project. We offered our prayers and words of advice, nothing more. It was not easy for Dave and me to step aside, but now we recognized why God had provided the man before providing the property. Inch by inch, John progressed in his efforts to obtain the estate in Garrison.

When he had done all the bargaining he could, John had the asking price down to $175,000. Also obtained was a concession whereby we had to make just one payment annually. That payment, however, was enough to floor us; it called for a sum of $15,000 to be paid each January for the next fifteen years or so until the remainder of our debt had been paid off. I was not used to such economics, but by this time the Lord had taught me that as long as we left things in His hands and didn't try to accomplish all things by ourselves, He would intercede for us in strange and wonderful ways. On the day that we signed the original bill of sale for the property in Garrison we committed the whole project into His keeping. We had to. There was no way that *we* could come up with $15,000 every January.

My faith grows more unshakable with each year, but I must admit that along about November of 1967 there came to our minds a thought about how we were going to meet our January payment. The year was eleven months old and we had not been able to set aside any funds. With each passing day, that $15,000 payment began to look more imposing. December came, and still no indication of how we could get the money, if we could get it at all. Surely the Lord wouldn't have us lose the property after having invested so much money and time in it already and especially not since our ministry among the women was now blossoming as we had always hoped it would.

As always, the Lord was faithful. Shortly before our deadline, we received notice from the United Foundation that we had been awarded a grant which would take care of our annual $15,000 payment until such time as the property was completely paid for. I slumped in my office chair and offered a prayer of thanks.

There was one request added to this grant by the United Foundation people, one we were glad they had been thoughtful enough to put there. They asked that we call the estate the Walter Hoving Home for Girls. We were happy to do so, for Walter Hoving, the chairman of the board of Tiffany's, has long been a member of the Teen Challenge board of advisors.

He has taken a sincere interest in our work and has cooperated to the fullest in helping us to acquire funds to continue our work.

An average of twenty girls live there now with the Bentons, and the tranquility of their new environment has worked wonders. No longer are the women as jittery or as troublesome as when they were in Brooklyn. A fringe benefit of being situated where they are is that the nuns in a nearby Catholic convent have invited the girls from our home to make use of their swimming pool.

One day shortly after we had purchased the estate, I went up there to spend an afternoon. There were only a few girls staying at the home then: four who had been mainlining with heroin (injecting it directly into the bloodstream) and one, a former gang "doll," who, at the tender age of 16, had become an unwed mother two weeks earlier. All five were standing on the flagstone terrace in front of the building as I walked by. It was a warm and sunny day and as I stopped to observe these girls, tigresses transplanted from the jungles of New York, I wondered how they might react to the beauty and grandeur which made up their new neighborhood.

"Wow," was all that one of the girls could say.

"I don't know," said another. "I just don't know about this place. It's just so beautiful that I don't know what to think."

Just then the baby began to cry. The mother picked him up carefully and held him in her arms. It was to no avail and the mother looked helplessly at her infant. One of the other girls walked briskly over to the baby, tenderly took him from his mother and began rocking him in her arms. It was still to no avail. The girl then softly but sternly said to the baby, "Shut up, brat, or I'll break your arm." They were words that had been offered strictly in jest, but they worked, and after a few moments of silence everyone laughed.

"See," said the girl who had quieted the child, "you gotta talk strict to these kids. I ought to know. I had a baby when I was 15."

As I walked away, I smiled at the realization that these girls were already undergoing a transformation. I knew that a few weeks ago a baby's cries would have been cause for them to have filled the air with four-letter words. The beauty that now surrounded them was having the desired tranquilizing effect. Their new environment was, without a doubt, a masterpiece of nature. In the foreground were sprawling lawns, flowerbeds in full glow, long rows of neatly trimmed hedges. A little further off were towering pines and clusters of weeping willows. And beyond all this were acres and acres of woodland. It bespoke solitude.

thirteen /...
···/ 74.7 percent

I N 1962 THE LATE John F. Kennedy had this to say about the
problem of drug addiction:

> There is no area in which there is so much mystery, so much
> misunderstanding and so many differences of opinion as in the
> area of narcotics. The discouragingly high degree of relapse
> among addicts who leave our medical institutions free of all
> physical dependence upon drugs is clear evidence that more
> must be done.

Not long ago, we made some tabulations of what had happened to addicts who had come to us over a three-year period.
Not giving our program any break, we counted all those who
were with us from as little as one day to those who stayed all
the way through our program. Thirty percent of those who
stayed with us from one day to a year had remained free of
drugs after leaving Teen Challenge. For those who went
through our entire program, the percentage of who did not
revert back to drugs was 74.7. Just how good is this? Well, we
know that our batting average is among the best in the world,
if not *the* best. I don't have statistics from other organizations,
but I do know that officials at the federal hospital in Lexington, Kentucky, which until recently had the largest staff and
most elaborate facilities in the world for working with addicts,
have often quoted their percentage of success, usually phrasing
it as, "two per cent, and sometimes we are not so sure about
those two per cent." There is a saying among narcotics agents
that they can count on 98 percent recidivism, which again in-

dicates that 2 percent of the so-called reformed addicts stay clean. This is what John F. Kennedy had in mind when he spoke of "the discouragingly high degree of relapse."

Logically, we at Teen Challenge should have the 2 percent success, for we have so many things going against us. We probably would have just 2 percent success except that we have one great thing going *for* us—the power of God—and we use it freely. I doubt that any of the other treatment centers in this country are as strapped for funds as we are, and I am sure that none of them has fewer trained personnel to care for the addicts than we do.

Many organizations prefer to work with addicts in a program that goes on for three or four years before they are sent back to rejoin society. Our program is a two-stage affair: the addict spends approximately three months at our Center in Brooklyn and then is transferred to our farm in Pennsylvania for further schooling and rehabilitation. In all, our program lasts approximately one year. In some places, the cost of sending an addict through a four-year program runs close to $20,000. For us, the cost for keeping a person is about $2,000 annually.

Back in 1964, Dr. Robert Baird of the Haven Clinic in Manhattan was asked by a *Time* reporter to comment on the Teen Challenge program. Said Dr. Baird: "What are they going to do—turn every addict in the country into a minister?" I can sympathize with Dr. Baird's feelings and I know that there are others who share with him the belief that addicts who come to Teen Challenge are cured of their addiction to narcotics by "religion."

There are times when I sit back and ponder what has been accomplished at the Center, and I realize that neither I nor anyone else can explain how or why we have been so successful. After all, we don't get *any* financial support from the federal government and we do not have *any* "professional" workers. When I think about this, I realize that the key to our success is that we do not offer the addicts "religion" but that we offer them the Bible and show them that Jesus is willing to help anyone at any time, no matter how hopeless a person may believe his life to be.

Although there is, undoubtedly, a certain amount of respect among all of us who are working with drug addicts, there are areas of disagreement. One of the strongest objections that we get from doctors and other trained personnel is that we do not have qualified people to care for drug addicts. This we do not dispute. Our rebuttal is that we have found that hours of prayer have been much more beneficial to our patients than hours of psychiatric treatment. This leads to the main bone of contention between our methods at Teen Challenge and those employed at other places. We know that whatever success we have had at Teen Challenge has come through the power of God. Hospitals and other centers for treating addicts have failed to recognize the single most important dimension of the people they are dealing with—their spiritual lives. (By the way, those doctors who used to scold us for using cold turkey are no longer as numerous or as vocal. Some, in fact, now prescribe it themselves.)

We have talked with many doctors who don't believe us when we tell them about the high percentage of cured patients we have had. These doctors have spent too many years in training for their profession to believe that upstarts like us can do what we have done. Here, again, they are overlooking the power of God and are trying to attribute to mere mortals that which the Lord has brought to pass.

These medically oriented people assail us by saying that we fail to spend long hours of probing to find out why a person is sick. What we are doing wrong, they inform us, is that we are curing our patients without first determining the cause of what we are trying to cure. This, they say, is impossible. All I can do is point to the hundreds of graduates we have as living proof that it *is* possible through God. One of our converts put it well when he said, "When I came to know the Lord, my parents didn't change, my society didn't change, my neighbors didn't change, but *I* changed, and that's why I am well."

Medical science is replete with complex terminology for the various ills that assault men. We prefer to keep things on a simpler, more understandable plane, referring to men's problems as sin. Don't get me wrong; we realize that lots of people have mental and physical disorders. It's just that we have come to the point where we understand that if a person can remove the overpowering effects of sin from his life he will, at the same time, get rid of other ailments with fancy-sounding names.

One of the most tragic statistics of our times is that between one-half and three-quarters of all the patients in American hospitals are there because of emotionally induced illnesses. The doctors who have arrived at these figures admit that people, in a very real sense, make themselves sick. This is also a fundamental concept of Christianity, which contends that men make themselves ill through sin. We have kept this in mind as we have conducted our work among drug addicts, for we have seen men cured physically shortly after they have been cured spiritually.

One of the techniques used most often by doctors is to let the addict know of the seriousness of his condition. I agree that it is good to be frank with a person, but I cannot believe that it is necessary or beneficial to keep saying to a drug user, "No matter how long you stay off drugs, you'll always be an addict at heart and there will always be a craving for drugs." To me that seems to be tantamount to telling the addict that he is going to be haunted for the remainder of his life by the one thing that he must escape if he hopes to live normally.

Our approach has been diametrically the opposite, not because we are trying to be different, but because we feel that it is in accordance with what the Bible teaches. In II Corinthians 5:17 (KJV) we are told: "Therefore if any man be in Christ, he is a new creature: old things are passed away; behold, all things are become new."

These drug addicts who have accepted Christ *must* have become new creatures; they certainly would never have invited the Lord into their lives if they were still the same sinful people they were in years gone by.

During one of the many sessions that a man named Benny spent with psychiatrists, he was told that the reason he had become a drug addict was because he had a hatred for his older brother. When Benny asked what he could do about this, he was told that he would have to replace this hatred with love. Just like that, in one stroke, Benny was to take hatred (which he did not feel existed) and transform it magically into love,

When Benny asked the psychiatrist how a person could achieve such a transition of emotions, he was given some vague advice on how to conjure up love. But he told us that once he accepted Christ, he found the love he had been seeking.

One of the most poignant case histories of a drug addict at Teen Challenge is that of Demetrio Rodriguez Jr., who is known to us as Demi. Let's have Demi's father give us the details of the first portion of his son's story.

"Looking back, I remember the day I told my wife brokenheartedly, 'There's no hope for our son. Let's leave him alone. Don't say anything to him; just give him anything he wants, because I know he hasn't much more time to live.'

"Demi passed through a series of nightmares. We knew it wouldn't be long before Demi would take an overdose. Already, he had attempted suicide twice, once when he tried to jump from a rooftop and once again when he was going to shoot himself. He looked like a corpse—emaciated, haggard.

"We loved Demi and we never let him down. Once, it cost us $200 to get him out of jail after he had been caught driving a car without a license. Another time, he stole some of my clothes and pawned them. The police picked him up and we went down and bailed him out again.

"Then came two trips to the hospital in Lexington, Kentucky. The first trip was a harrowing experience. On the way to Kentucky, Demi shot up. The authorities placed him in a sanatorium in Columbus, Ohio, because he had acted so strangely on the train. My wife and I traveled three days in my cab to Columbus to sign him out. It took us three more days to drive him from Columbus to Lexington. On the way, Demi tried to slash his wrists. We didn't dare leave him alone at night for fear that he would jump from a window. No sleep for three nights.

"That first visit to Lexington was a failure. Demi was back on drugs as soon as he returned to New York City. After the second visit, Demi didn't want to return home because he said he had already caused us too much heartache. A psychiatrist at Lexington recommended Teen Challenge as a place where he could stay for a week or so until he found a job."

We had been in contact with the authorities in Lexington and were awaiting Demi's arrival. He had been at K.Y. for six months, but no sooner had he stepped off the train at Pennsylvania Station than he heard an inner voice urging him to go out and get high. Demi slid into a phone booth and called our number. When I answered the phone, Demi asked if it would be all right if he went home for a day and came to see us the next morning. I was tempted to say yes, but I knew that he most likely would go out and shoot up with heroin and that he would be lucky if he got home at all.

"No," I told Demi. "I think it would be better if you came over right now."

Demi picked up his bags and headed for a subway that would take him to Clinton Avenue. When he arrived he stood in front of our building. He was restless; he could feel the tug of the old life pulling at him and he wanted to give in. Demi walked away. Then he came back and stood in front of our Center. Again he walked away, and again he returned. At long last, Demi summoned the courage to walk through the door.

Demi told us that while he had been in K.Y. the doctors had informed him that he was pretty much of a hopeless case. They told him that maybe, just maybe, a new wonder drug might help him. It was dangerous, they warned Demi, and he would have to sign a release form so that the hospital would not be responsible if anything happened to him. Demi took one of the pills containing the wonder drug. Soon he began seeing pink elephants and an assortment of grotesque beings. It was a frightening experience. No more pills for Demi.

Shortly before Demi left Lexington, a psychiatrist spoke to him. As always, Demi had hopes that he might get something out of such a session. What he got was this bit of advice: "Young man, there is only one way you are going to be cured of drug addiction and that's for you to walk out of here and let a truck run over you."

It wasn't long after Demi came to Teen Challenge that he accepted Christ as his Savior, and the happiness that was his he has shared with his mother and father, both of whom have also given their lives to Jesus.

fourteen /...
···/ from copenhagen, denmark
/ to martinsville, indiana

THE MINISTRY OF Teen Challenge extends far beyond Clinton Avenue, reaching into areas of life and corners of the globe which no one dared to dream of when Dave first came to New York. Aside from our home for the girls, our school, and our farm, we also have a full-fledged ministry among the hippies and beatniks in Greenwich Village. There are also other Teen Challenge Centers in cities such as San Francisco, Los Angeles, Phoenix, Chicago, Philadelphia, Detroit, Dallas, Denver, Toronto, and another in Bayamon, just outside of San Juan, Puerto Rico. We were particularly pleased that some of the workers at the Los Angeles Center when it first opened up were men who had gone through our program in Brooklyn. And we take continuing pleasure in noting that other Brooklyn converts are laboring in Centers all across the country, in Canada, and in Puerto Rico.

Nicky Cruz, one of the first gang members who came to salvation under Dave's ministry in Brooklyn, has established Outreach for Youth in Oakland, California. His goal is to reach pre-teenagers.

There is still much more to our outreach than this. In 1968 we embarked upon a radio ministry. Furthermore, Dave conducts crusades and youth rallies and speaks to various groups around the world—from Copenhagen, Denmark, to Johannesburg, South Africa; from Darmstadt, Germany, to Stockholm, Sweden; from London, England, to Anaheim, California.

Sometimes we feel we have gone as far as we can possibly go. No sooner do we get such thoughts, however, than another door is opened. Right now we are planning to add yet another phase to our work by starting a Peace Corps-type program in New York, a person-to-person ministry in which people would live in the neighborhoods with the folks they are trying to minister to. In this way, we feel that these needy ones would be able to come to our representatives on a more informal basis. Some people, we know, balk at the thought of coming to Teen Challenge because they feel they will be swallowed up by a large organization. What they want is to just sit down and talk out their problems. Our objective in such a program would not be to set up chapels or churches, but rather to let everyone know that he is welcome to come to the apartment of our workers for advice or counseling or merely to have a chat.

Many of our staff members take part in outside work, mostly as guest speakers. A group of our workers went to a church in upstate New York a few years ago and they came back with a revealing story. It seems that after they had spoken at the church that Sunday they had given an altar call, inviting any and all people who wished to confess their sins and accept salvation through Christ Jesus to come forward. No one stirred. Later, outside the church, though, three young boys and two girls spoke to one of our staffers. All five teenagers had the same question: What is meant by confession and salvation?

It was explained to these youngsters that "all have sinned and come short of the glory of God," and that if anyone sought forgiveness and believed that Jesus was the Son of God and his personal Savior, then salvation was his for the asking. Salvation, they were told, was a gift from Jesus, who died on the cross that all men's sins might be forgiven, and that He had made it available to all people who believed in Him. Christ and the salvation that He offered to all mankind were gifts from God intended to remove the burden of sin and to give men everywhere a new hope for living, our workers explained. All five youngsters said right then and there that they believed that Jesus was the son of God and that they wanted to be saved. It was a rather unusual occurrence and yet, as is always true when someone receives Christ into his life, it was a tender and beautiful one.

Dave has had exceptional results from his evangelistic efforts, particularly among young people. He likes to refer to these youngsters as "goodniks," believing that they are far from being as bad as they are sometimes portrayed. Billy Graham once made the statement that he knew of no one who better had the ear of young people than Dave. I agree. Dave has had such an enthusiastic response wherever he has gone that he is able to spend very little time at the Center. So extensive has his itinerary become that he has had to set up a small office near his home in Massapequa Park, Long Island, to coordinate his meetings and crusades.

Dave has been gone for months at a time on his trips. The two of us made a trip to South Africa in 1968, and after having traveled almost halfway around the world, we finally had the chance to sit down and talk to one another face to face. Because Dave does so much traveling, the board of directors of Teen Challenge appointed me as director of our Center in Brooklyn in December of 1966. Dave still oversees the work in its entirety, though.

In a way, it is good that Dave doesn't spend more time at the office than he does. He gets like a bucking bronco when he is cooped up behind a desk. Administrative work is one thing for which Dave has little taste. He is too restless, too energetic, to sit for any long periods of time. It upset him a bit, however, that he was no longer able to keep tabs on every little thing that was going on. Once we were able to convince him that there were those of us who were willing to handle the paper work so that he could carry on his gifted ministry with young people, though, he seemed to feel much more reconciled to this reapportionment of responsibilities.

During my early years in the work lots of people, knowing that Dave, Mom, Cindy and I all worked at the Center, would refer to us as "a Wilkerson outfit." Comments such as this used to bother Dave. He didn't want to be guilty of showing favoritism toward members of his own family—and, believe me, he did not show any toward us. Mom and Cindy fit right into their secretarial jobs and helped with street work and in our Greenwich Village coffeehouses. I was the source of most of the irritation about our being "a Wilkerson outfit," for I am certain that many people felt that the only reason I was there was because I was Dave's brother. It is true that because of our close relationships, I was aware almost from the first of what he was attempting to accomplish among the young people of New York. I can honestly say, however, that the position I now hold as director of Teen Challenge in Brooklyn was not handed to me because I am a Wilkerson.

If anything, Dave made things harder on me than he did on most of the other members of our staff. There were times when I felt that he was being overly cautious about this situation and that he was sidelining me so that people would stop pointing fingers our way.

Mom has always had a vital part in our ministry. During our early years in Brooklyn some of the men in our program who were hesitant about talking to Dave or to me would go to Mom with their problems. More recently, Mom has been the driving force behind our ministry in Greenwich Village. Mom is a gentle person, but she has been right in the middle of the thickest trouble at times and has never flinched. It all began in 1961 when the Villagers became upset because city officials and police tried to keep them from congregating in large groups. Villagers had a habit not only of congregating, but of making a considerable din when they got together. Well, the more the city fathers asked for quiet and the more the police tried to bring about that quiet, the louder things got.

Mom used to go down to the Village on Sunday afternoons, and it was while she was there on one of her visits that she passed out some Christian literature and began answering questions put to her by a group of law students. They were in a mood to try out their powers of argumentation and figured that Mom looked like a soft touch, so they began peppering her with questions about Christianity—and she began rattling off answers that soon made it apparent that she knew what she was talking about. Before long, a large group had gathered around Mom. As soon as the policemen saw a crowd forming, they came on the double. When they found that Mom was the cause of it all they told her that she couldn't go around doing things like this.

"I can't help it," Mom told the policemen. "I began by

speaking to a few boys and all of a sudden all these others gathered around to listen. I can't stop them from doing that."

On a number of occasions a policeman would tell Mom, "If you don't stop passing out that literature, we're going to have to run you in."

"Okay," Mom would say. "Get your paddy wagon ready."

"You're too willing," the patrolman would reply as he shook his head and walked away.

Our ministry in Greenwich Village has in more recent years been centered in a small chapel which we have there. Our present one, called The Lost Coin and located at 190 Sullivan Street, is a block and a half from our original outpost. The first Teen Challenge establishment in the Village was known as the Catacomb Chapel and was right on McDougal Street. It had been called the Den of the 40 Thieves by its previous owner. The purpose in getting a place such as this was to set up a coffeehouse which we hoped would attract the crowds of young people who wander so aimlessly around the area. The ministry has lived up to its expectations; during the two and a half years that we ran our Catacomb Chapel we did a landslide business.

I'd better clarify what I mean by "business." Our business, no matter where we are, is serving Christ and presenting His message of salvation. Our coffeehouse was unlike the others in the Village. All we had to offer was a few crackers, some coffee and soft drinks. We didn't charge anything for our refreshments. Village regulars soon came to know that our Catacomb Chapel was a place where they could sit in peace. They knew that we wanted to engage them in conversation about the Bible and Christianity and that evangelism was our goal. This, I am happy to report, deterred few of them from coming back again and again. Visitors to the Village also crowded into our coffeehouse. Business was excellent, so much so that we were driven out of our location. People would wait on the steps leading into the chapel or sit on the railing around the steps or wait on the sidewalk, sometimes in such numbers that nearby merchants would complain that other people did not patronize their stores because they couldn't get around the throngs. It didn't take long before our landlord notified us that there would be a considerable boost in our rent. His rate of increase was out of our financial reach, and it was with a touch of sadness that we closed the door of the Catacomb Chapel for the last time.

There is nothing fancy about The Lost Coin, which opened in the summer of 1966. There are about a dozen tables and booths and enough seats for some fifty people, and instead of offering passersby some loud and lively entertainment, Mom can only offer quiet conversation. But people want to talk and Mom is always ready to listen. She has a way with people, and her warm smile doesn't exactly scare customers away. Watching how she deals with her customers is a lesson in itself.

How Mom worked with Stanley is an example of what I mean. Stanley was a Jewish boy with an active and intelligent mind. He was also a beatnik. Stanley started coming in to talk to Mom and her helpers several years ago, and he kept coming back week after week. Each time he came he stayed for hours, eagerly discussing portions of the Bible from the Old Testament and the New Testament as well. Stanley told Mom the first time he stopped in that he was an agnostic, a statement he made a point of making every time he came by over a period of several months.

Well, Mom told her workers one night that they were not to bother with Stanley any more. She felt that he had been told about the gospel often enough and that there were others who were coming through her doors who had not yet been spoken to. Some of Mom's helpers may not have agreed with her approach; yet they respected her and were obedient to her orders. They also obeyed her second order concerning Stanley, which was that they should all pray that the words that had been uttered to this young man would take root in his heart and that he might finally understand.

It didn't take Stanley long to realize that he had been ostracized, but he still kept showing up. He figured that if no one would talk to him the next best thing to do was to seat himself at a table where one of the workers was chatting with someone else. For the first few nights, Stanley just sat and listened. Before long, though, Stanley began wriggling into the conversations. It all began when one of the workers was trying to quote a verse from the Bible and couldn't remember all the words. Stanley knew the verse, so he spoke up. After a night or two of this, Stanley became more and more engrossed in the conversations in which he invited himself to join. Soon he found that he was defending the Bible and Christianity.

Stanley was surprised by what he had done, and he admitted to Mom and to the other workers that he felt a strange satisfaction about his behavior. "But I'm still an agnostic and don't think I'll ever change," he would say as he left. They kept telling him over and over, "We're praying for you. We're praying that the Lord will bring you to salvation." One night Stanley came back with a new statement: "I finally understood what you were all talking about and I have given my heart to the Lord."

Mom has always been blessed with plenty of helpers in this ministry, including one or more members of our staff at the Center who are always assigned to duty in the Village on those nights when The Lost Coin is open. Our hours at The Lost Coin reflect the ebb and flow of the Village: from 8 P.M. until midnight on Thursday, Friday and Saturday and from 6 P.M. until 9:30 P.M. on Sunday night.

Of Mom's many faithful helpers none has been more diligent nor lasted longer than Fay Mianulli, who grew up in the Village. When Fay learned that we were setting up a program she wrote to Mom and asked if she could lend a hand. Fay, who also works in the mailroom at the Center, has been lending a hand ever since.

"The Village is a weekend place," Mom says. "People come to look at the beatniks and the hippies and to walk around. We have people who come to help us in our work from New Jersey, Rhode Island, Connecticut. They like to roam the streets and witness to the folks and they like to bring them back to The Lost Coin so they can sit down and talk some more to them.

"As for the people of the Village, I don't mind them at all. If I were not a Christian, I think I might be one of them. I have a searching mind. So many of them are searching. An awful lot come from broken homes and some of them complain to me, 'I have prayed to God to help my folks to live together and to get along, but He doesn't answer.' I tell them,

Mom Wilkerson and Fay Mianulli in earnest dialogue with gentleman outside The Lost Coin coffee house in Greenwich Village. *Below:* Dave and Don Wilkerson take part in radio interview.

'Maybe God is waiting for you so that he can work through you if you will only allow yourself to become a fit vessel for His use.' These people are seeking answers. They have done a lot of thinking about their problems and they have intelligent questions to ask.

"A lot of Bible school students who have worked with me ask, 'Why don't we get tough questions like that in school?' I tell them, 'It's a good education working here because you have to go back and read your Bible and get to know it if you want to help these people.' "

Another of our ministries is in the field of radio. We had been thinking for a few years about the possibilities of putting together some sort of radio program, but we didn't have the time, funds, or qualifications to do so. Then along came John Fester. John came to us one day and said that he had done some work as a radio engineer and that he thought perhaps it was time for us to consider having a Teen Challenge radio show. The idea was appealing, so we told John to stick around and help us pray about it. Before long, John built a recording studio and a separate room in which to house equipment for it at 444.

Once that was done, it was my task to see if we actually could do some programming. Dave wanted to lend a hand, but when he became too busy with other things I plunged ahead on my own. What I wanted to do was to come up with programs that could be tape recorded at our Center and distributed to radio stations around the country. First, I got a list of the addresses of the stations that might use such a show. Then it was time to write a script and tape a program so that the people at these stations would have an idea of what sort of show we would be able to offer. Never having written a script before, I was afraid to get my hopes up too high when I sent out the first batch of audition tapes.

It wasn't long, though, before I received a letter of acceptance from Station WCPK in Martinsville, Indiana. A woman at the station wrote that she was familiar with the work of Teen Challenge and that she had been contributing regularly to our support. When I finished reading the letter, I let out a big sigh.

As much as anything, I was pleased that the first station to accept was in a small town such as Martinsville, Indiana. Then I realized I didn't have the faintest idea of how big or small it really was or even where it was located. I went to the road atlas and looked up Martinsville. For a minute, I thought the whole thing might have been a gag: I couldn't find any Martinsville in Indiana. Then I spotted it, about 20 miles southwest of Indianapolis. I put a circle next to it so that it wouldn't be so hard to find the next time. Then I looked up the population. It was listed as 8,476. I got goose bumps thinking about this little town and how suddenly it had become so meaningful to those of us at Teen Challenge.

Within a few days, our show was also picked up by KMOF-FM in St. Paul, Minnesota, and by WSAE, a station in Spring Arbor, Michigan. Within four months our weekly half-hour program was being carried regularly by fifteen stations. Before long we were producing two shows a week. One, called *Youth In A Fix,* is geared to stimulate Christians into action. Our other show, *Youth Beat,* challenges non-Christians by pointing out to them their need for salvation.

During those early months our expenses were heavy, but our financial worries were eased in several ways. A number of stations carried our programs without charging us for the air time and others cut their fees. And listeners began sending us donations. As I was going through the mail one day, my eyes suddenly bulged; someone had sent us a check for $500 to help us carry on our radio ministry. I looked to see where the check had come from. When I saw the postmark on the envelope, I couldn't keep from smiling. It was from Martinsville, Indiana.

fifteen /...
···/ our gang

WHAT WE NEED AROUND here is a carpenter," I said one day to John Benton, who was also aware of the thousand-and-one repair jobs that had to be taken care of in our five buildings on Clinton Avenue. I would have done some of the work myself, but when it comes to carpentry I have a unique ability to saw boards at never-before-seen angles, bend nails with a hammer, measure incorrectly, and wind up with an end product that looks like something out of a Rube Goldberg cartoon. The more that we talked about our need for a carpenter, the more we realized that was all we were doing—talking.

"There's only one way to settle this," John said at last, "and that's to pray about it."

Pray we did, and so did others who learned of our need. Shortly after we had begun praying, a young man named David Brett walked into the Center. He said that he was from New Zealand, that he had just dropped out of Bible school, and that he was hoping he could stay with us until his folks were able to send money for him to return home. Before I was able to tell him politely that this was out of the question, he said, "I'd be here only a few weeks and I'd want to work while I was here. I can paint and I can do carpentry."

Carpentry. It was as if someone had pushed a button that had set off a siren. "If you can do carpentry work, you've got a job," I told Dave. "We'll give you room and board and a hammer."

It was soon evident that Dave was no ordinary carpenter; he was a craftsman. When he cut a board, it was cut straight.

150

And he didn't miss when he hammered nails, nor did he measure one side of a board longer than the other. My only regret was that Dave was going to be with us for only a few weeks—or so we thought. First it was the failure of his money to arrive that kept Dave from leaving us. Then his visa expired and we sent him to Canada on one of those roundabout missions designed to cut through heaps of red tape, a journey that took him to see some friends of ours who had a friend who handled visas up there. It all went quite smoothly. There was more than enough work for Dave at the Center, so he stayed with us a little longer. That was two years ago. He is still with us. Here is Dave's account of what he has been doing since he came to Teen Challenge.

"I did carpentry work for about four months, day and night, but I wanted to have more of an active ministry. About the only thing I was doing along those lines was to preach in chapel on Saturday mornings. Then Dave came to me and asked me to pray about driving the Go-Ye Mobile that was being used for outside ministries and I was very happy when that opened up. I was put in charge of that all summer and we went out every afternoon and every night with a team of workers on the streets.

"One day I felt led to go to a particular place in Brooklyn, to a community center in Brownsville that I had tried to get into before but had not been permitted to enter. I had seven girls with me that night and I was the only fellow. You are supposed to be a member to get into the center, but this time I was allowed to go inside. After distributing tracts to the kids in there—there were maybe fifty of them—I went outside, got the girls, and we all went back in. We took over the whole center. Everything came to a halt: they stopped playing pool, they turned off the record player, they stopped playing all their games. In a matter of minutes we had Bible study groups going all over the place. About seven or eight kids accepted the Lord that night.

"The man in charge of the place couldn't believe his eyes. He just stood by the door for an hour and a half, and when we left he said he had never seen anything like this. These were wild kids. Most of them were in the habit of sniffing glue and smoking pot and taking pills. Anyway, we went back a week later with a movie. More than a hundred kids were there. They were sitting on the pool tables, anywhere they could find a place. Nine more young boys gave their lives to the Lord that night. From then on we went there every week.

"I told a friend of mine that I wished we could have a church now that we had started a work among the young people in that area. It seemed like a far-off dream, but I reminded myself that if it was a desire that met with the Lord's will He would bring it to pass. I knew that it was not something I could go around and openly ask for. Right after we had finished our summer evangelism Don asked me, 'Would you like to start a church in Brownsville?'

"I drove all around the neighborhood looking for a proper place, but the best I could find was one that seated only about forty or fifty people. Still, this was the only one I felt right about. It was $90 a month. I spoke to Don about the place and said, 'If they'll give us a month's rent free would it be all right to take it?' He said it would. I didn't tell the landlord I wanted a month's rent free. I asked him, 'Would you buy me the paint free if I fix the place up?'

" 'I'll tell you what,' he said. 'I'll give you a month's rent free.'

"The first night I was there—I was working with another fellow from Teen Challenge—a bunch of local boys came in. 'Whatcha doin'?' they asked. 'What's happenin', man?'

" 'We're going to have a little church for you guys,' I said.

"They said, 'Oh yeah?' They must have noticed the Go-Ye Mobile outside because they wanted to know if we were from Teen Challenge. When we assured them that we were, they told us that some of them had been to our meetings at the community center. 'We'll come,' they said. 'We like Teen Challenge. In fact, all the Rats will come.'

" 'Who's the rats?' I wanted to know.

" 'That's our gang, man,' they told me.

"Every night that I worked there fixing up the place, about four or five of these Rats would show up in their good clothes— even their leather jackets—and would help out and would get paint all over themselves. They had never painted before. Because they helped me in getting the place ready, I think they felt it was more like their place; they really felt like they were a part of something for once.

"The night that we opened the place we had twenty-six young people in. Six of them made *real* decisions for the Lord. We started Bible studies rather than social times. We tried to have social activities, but they just didn't work. We've found it much more profitable to study the Bible."

Most of the people who live in Brownsville, which is one of the few areas in Brooklyn where gangs still exist, are Puerto Rican. I was dubious about Dave's renting the place there that he did, especially since there was a lively numbers racket in operation right downstairs. But Dave has an engaging way about him and the local youths took a liking to him. They took pride in being able to help fix up the place and they liked to watch over it when he wasn't around. They frequently tell us, "We'll watch the place for you and if anybody tries anything we'll take care of them for you."

It wasn't long after the place had been all fixed up, though, that trouble erupted. The first thing that happened was that someone stole some money from the men who ran the numbers racket. In the moments of confusion that followed, the owners of the numbers operation ran out to the street. Their No. 1 suspect was Dave, whom they had just seen drive away. Then their attention was diverted to a brand new Pontiac which was parked at the curb. These people are familiar with everything and everyone on their block and when they realized that they had never seen the Pontiac before, they determined that it belonged to the man who had robbed them. To get even, they set the car on fire. A few weeks after that, another fire gutted the building where Dave had set up his base of operations.

It seemed like a big loss but, as it turned out, Dave had done such a good job of getting Teen Challenge accepted in Brownsville that we have been able to carry on the work without renting any apartment. Members of our staff now conduct Bible studies in the homes of people in Brownsville, and throughout the week they minister to them in many ways.

Our workers visit the local community centers, counsel with people and bring groups of youngsters to the Center for services. And what about Dave? Well, he has graduated from Brownsville and has been placed in charge of a new teen outreach in Atlantic Highlands, New Jersey.

During one of Dave's visits to the community center in Brownsville in the summer of 1967, he had an unexpected visitor—New York Mayor John Lindsay. The mayor, who was on one of his tours around New York, popped in without any advance notice. He was curious about the activities that went on in such community centers; when he began asking questions, Dave and some of the other staff members explained what they were doing there and what Teen Challenge represented. This was one of the rare nights when Dave had taken along a stack of copies of *The Cross and the Switchblade*. It is too costly to give them away every time that he goes out, but this time he had felt led to do so and was able to give copies to Mayor Lindsay and his aides.

A few days later, one of our workers wrote a letter to the mayor in which he further explained the role of Teen Challenge and invited him to visit us. About a week after that, there came a telephone call from one of Mayor Lindsay's aides saying that the mayor would be coming to Teen Challenge for a look at 6 P.M. on August 3. In the meantime, though, race riots began springing up around the country and Mayor Lindsay was appointed by President Lyndon Johnson to a panel that was to investigate the situation. As a result, Mayor Lindsay has not yet been able to visit us. We have been promised a visit in the future.

The Go-Ye Mobile that Dave Brett spoke about is a Chevrolet van that was donated to us by the T. L. Osborn Evangelistic Association of Tulsa, Oklahoma. We have called it the Go-Ye Mobile because we use it in connection with our evangelistic efforts. The name itself has been taken from the Bible: "Go ye into all the world, and preach the gospel to every creature" (Mark 16:15, KJV). Dave, utilizing his talents as a carpenter once again, has installed wooden benches in the rear of the Go-Ye Mobile and has built in cabinets to carry supplies of books and tracts. Even more important has been Dave's work outside of the Go-Ye Mobile. He has conducted innumerable street rallies and a wide variety of other activities that I am certain he never dreamed of becoming involved in when he first walked into the Center seeking "a place to stay for a few weeks."

That is not all there is to the story of David Brett. His whole family—mother, father, sister, and wife (the former Charlene Kluck, who was already a secretary at Teen Challenge when she and Dave met)—all work for Teen Challenge. This means that the Bretts outnumber the Wilkersons in full-time workers by a margin of five to three. Someone got off a bad pun about this situation by saying that our slogan should be, "Give us this day our daily Brett." All I can say is that I am pleased to have every one of the Bretts with us and I hope that nobody starts to snarl and call us "a Brett outfit."

Where do we get the rest of our workers? Well, they come from a variety of places—from Missouri and Oklahoma, from Tennessee and Oregon, from Ohio and North Dakota. Quite a few have read *The Cross and the Switchblade,* have been stirred by the boldness of my brother's faith, and have come to us feeling that they will be able to impress us by trying to exude a similar attitude. Scores of people are attracted by what they feel is the glamor of working with addicts and delinquents. This is especially true of young people in their late teens. A number of people with hardly any finances have driven long distances to come to us. They arrive confidently at our door, just as if to say, "Well, here we are." They sincerely feel they have been sent by the Lord. I don't think that we have ever accepted anyone under these circumstances. We have felt that they were led more by their own personal zeal and goodheartedness than anything else.

To beef up our staff for the summer, we bring in a number of college students, but whether they are with us for the summer or on a permanent basis, all our workers have to do much more than evangelize. This was a lesson that I, too, had to learn. Perhaps the hardest adjustment for me to make was to swallow my pride and understand that I would have to lay aside my own preaching ministry so that I could work shoulder to shoulder with the rest of the staff. Occasionally, I get a chance to do some preaching, but most of the work at Teen Challenge is built around counseling and, in some instances, administrative duties.

For the most part, our best workers are those who come from small towns. I think this is because these people are accustomed to doing menial chores and because they don't have the calloused outlook that blinds so many city dwellers, robbing them of much of their compassion and their ability to see beyond themselves. Actually, very few of the workers we have had have not been satisfactory. Their loyalty, their willingness to give of themselves, and their ability to grit their teeth and work hard have amazed me. In a land overflowing with rebellious youth, it has been rewarding to find so many who have remained steadfast in their desire to help others.

It takes a while for these youngsters, most of whom have never seen a ghetto or a drug addict, to adjust to life in Brooklyn. Whether they come with it or not, all of them pass through a period in which they experience a certain amount of fear. They survive because they come feeling a burden of interest and concern for the work and a willingness to yield themselves to the Lord. Although some have been given good scares, not one has left us because of fear. Some of the girls have led such sheltered lives that they don't comprehend the dangers suddenly swirling all around them. In the average middle-class environment it is natural for boys and girls to talk and mingle with one another and yet keep their distance, but in Brooklyn, if a girl is nice to one of the addicts on the street, he sometimes interprets this in the wrong way.

Back in the days when we had our Surfside Chapel at Coney Island, I noticed one boy who came and watched and listened night after night. I kept waiting for the night when he would indicate that our message was getting through to him. After five or six nights, he made his move, although it was hardly the kind I had been anticipating. "I'll get saved," he said, "if you'll get me a date with that chick up on the stage."

During the past few summers, we have used only small teams of workers, for we have found that this enables us to devote less time to teaching them *how* to reach the needy and to spend more time *doing* the reaching.

When I consider the wage scale at Teen Challenge it seems absurd that anyone would want to work for us. Salaries for summer employees are dependent upon our financial status at that moment. There have been times when we have been able to pay as high as $15 a week, but there have also been summers when we have not been able to pay *anything*. The wage scale for those who work for us full time is considerably higher, though I must admit that I am using the word "considerably" in a rather loose way. Staffers get $25 a week and usually receive a $5-a-month raise after three months. If both husband and wife are working, each starts at $25 and after three months or so is raised to $30.

Despite our small salaries, I believe that our workers are better off financially than most people earning ten, twenty, or more times than they. Everyone at Teen Challenge *knows* that he will get three square meals a day, will have living quarters, won't have to worry about paying for heat, electricity, water or gas, and won't have to fret about waking up with a hangover. Where else can you get a job where fringe benefits exceed the salary?

Some people have left high-salaried jobs at other places to work for us. It is hard to explain to those who worship the almighty dollar rather than the Almighty how a person can leave a $10,000-a-year job to work for some $1,500 a year. Men might perhaps better be able to fathom such cases if they were to turn their lives around and worship Christ with the same fervor with which they worship the dollar.

Another of our workers was Al Palmquist, who used to be our dean of men. Al was inexperienced at working with addicts and he had a roughness about him that made me wonder if he would fit in. His, fortunately, proved to be a good kind of roughness. When he would find a fellow who was cantankerous, Al would say to him, "Behave, or I'll throw you out." Nobody had to ask Al what he meant by statements such as that. And nobody was going to test Al's ability to toss someone out on his ear: Al is 6 foot 3, weighs 205 pounds and if he doesn't feel like throwing a person out the door he just might use his size 12 shoes to kick him out. He came to us in 1965, and this is how he described his work:

"One of my main jobs is to interview every fellow who comes off the street and wants to be admitted into our program. Maybe we'll have two beds open and twenty-five men who want to get in. That means picking two men out of that group. I weigh a lot of factors and once the men are admitted I try to keep very close tabs on how they are doing spiritually. Judging a man's sincerity is almost impossible. So often the ones you think can't possibly last turn out to be the best of all.

"An addict finds it hard to be on time over a period of days. Usually he'll start looking for a shot first thing when he gets up in the morning. Often he has committed his first crime of the day by eight in the morning and is on the way to a pawn shop so he can get money for a fix. Knowing this, I will sometimes put an obstacle in front of a boy to see how sincere he is about wanting to come in. I'll tell him he has to come to chapel three days in a row before I'll let him into the program. One fellow I told to come every day for a week did just that and I accepted him. Some of the ones I think are real smart alecks I tell to come to chapel and bring ten dollars for the building fund. Most of them don't show up, but those who are desperate find a way to drag themselves to the service and also find a way to come up with the ten dollars; they always do for drugs. Those who are this sincere, I give the ten dollars back to.

"I found one fellow named Shippy lying in the street one night all strung out from drugs. He was like a lot of other guys who look at me and see how big I am and the size of my feet—they think I'm a cop. He takes one look at me and moans, 'Oh, what'd I do now?' I talked to him about the Lord. Since then, he's brought lots of others to the Lord himself.

"It's hard to believe that the dirty, strung-out guy you see lying in the gutter is potentially a fine missionary, but we've seen it happen too often to ever give up on anyone."

I would like to have one more person, a young man named Bob Combs, present a few of his views about his work at Teen Challenge.

"My first assignment was to take lots of pictures of the

girls' home in Garrison for a photo album. I took the pictures, but I felt that it was a waste of time and that the albums in which they were arranged would just sit on someone's bookshelf and gather dust. The albums were presented to the United Foundation and this apparently helped in getting the Foundation to decide to give $15,000 yearly until the mortgage on the girls' home is paid off. Brother Benton says that without the pictures we probably wouldn't have gotten anything. This was a tremendous encouragement to me. The whole grant will be worth about $175,000, so I feel that I have been of some help.

"Most major magazines today have carried articles on drug addiction and you see so many of these stories that you figure, 'Well, this is something pretty distant.' I thought that the magazines were sensationalizing, but once I got here I found out that they had been telling the story pretty much as it was.

"Some of these boys have taken me back to their old neighborhoods where they still have friends who are addicted. They go back so they can tell these people what God has done for them. Their friends just look at them. They can't believe that here is a guy who just a year ago was shooting up drugs with them. They say that they can see the joy and the peace in the faces of converts like Simon and Tony and they become curious and these guys will come into the program. This is one of the reasons the program is so successful: these guys leave here and they really go on to live for the Lord. The guys on the outside see friends kick drugs, something that's supposed to be next to impossible."

A number of the people who work for us are not a part of our staff. Some of our converts have even done work for us while behind bars. Esther, a $100-a-night call girl from Manhattan, had accepted Christ at Teen Challenge. She had a six-month sentence to serve in a Brooklyn jail and, even though she could have gained a suspended sentence, Esther chose to serve out her time because she knew that she would literally have a captive audience to whom she could present her Christian testimony. By the time her six months were up, Esther had led several of the women in jail to the Lord.

Another volunteer was Doris Akers, a vocalist, arranger and songwriter who is known as Miss Gospel Music. She came to the Center one day in 1967 and sang at one of our chapel services. Doris is a sprightly and energetic woman, and when she had finished singing she lined up all the men in the audience at the front of the chapel. Then, one by one, she had them sing out, "Hello." After getting some idea of their voices, she arranged them in choir-fashion and had them vocalize as a group. Several of the staffers came up to my office—I was buried under a stack of paper work and had not been able to attend—to tell me about it in excited tones. I made it a point to have dinner with Miss Akers in the cafeteria that night to thank her for what she had done. She said that she enjoyed that type of work and that if she could be of assistance in any way for a week or two she would be glad to help out. When I suggested that the place where she could be of the most help was the farm, she said she would be glad to go there.

Once she got to the farm, she got all the boys together, picked out the best singers and formed a choir. She has a unique ability for working with people of this type. If someone would sing off key, Doris would walk over to him and playfully bop him on top of the head. Most of the men at the farm are Spanish and don't speak English, so she had to spend a lot of time teaching them the words to the songs. At one point during a rehearsal I was watching, she wanted to know, "How do you say 'silence' in Spanish?" One of the boys told her that "silencio" was the word she was after.

"Aw," said Doris, "I like my way better: shut up."

She did such a fine job with the choir that we took the group to a recording studio and produced an entire album. There is a noticeable absence of what might be called the "professional touch" to the songs, but this is easy to overlook when you realize that they are being sung by a group of former drug addicts who are now praising God with their voices.

As for our regular workers, one of them described the work load at the Center by saying, "A day off for a Teen Challenge staff worker is like a week's vacation with pay for a union laborer."

One of our workers came back to the Center after a long

and fruitless night of street ministry and said, "Tonight I learned a lesson about how easy it is to be misunderstood. I was talking to a young boy about the love that God has for each of us. I told this boy, 'I want you to know that I love you, too.' He looked at me suspiciously and then said, 'Man, either you are crazy or you're a homosexual.' "

Working at Teen Challenge is a strenuous job, one filled with unexpected events that rob workers of precious hours of sleep and days off. Hearing someone complain, however, is rare. There is too much rejoicing about the blessings for us to be overly concerned about the mishaps. One of the most frequently heard comments at Teen Challenge is that the work has done more for us than we have done for it. God has not only done a work *through* our staffers, but *in* them. It has been an experience in itself just to watch the transformation in the lives of our workers. They have come with a burden in their hearts, with a commitment, and with a love, all of which have been deepened at the Center. I think that every one of us can say that after working at Teen Challenge our values in life undergo a drastic change. When you live next to human need and you see people who have so little in their lives, the financial filigree of life loses its appeal.

sixteen /...
···/ and now for a word
/ from our sponsors

TEEN CHALLENGE OWES its very existence to the financial gifts and prayers of people all over the world and to the grace of God, who has motivated these men, women and children to be so faithful to us in their giving and praying. Down through the years, we have had some large donations, some of them from W. Clement Stone, some from other people, including a few we had never heard of. Teen Challenge as we know it today would certainly not be flourishing as it is if it were not for these donations. In all sincerity, though, I can say that the dollars and pennies that trickle in are equally appreciated for the faithfulness in which they were given and the sacrifices that people have made to help us.

In addition to those sponsors who have given large sums, we are dependent upon more than 25,000 others who faithfully send us from one to ten dollars. There are also church groups and other organizations that send in donations. And there are those who send us nickels and dimes and pennies. When I have the time, I like to open some of the mail and read the notes and letters that people send with their contributions. One elderly woman sent us her entire Social Security check of some sixty dollars one month; she included a note which said, "I know it's not a lot, but I just feel I have to do something." To me, this is very moving. So, too, are the letters that come from groups of youngsters who explain that the money they are enclosing has been raised by washing cars or mowing lawns or by doing some painting or snow-shoveling.

Receiving large grants has, in a way, been detrimental

to our fund raising. When people hear about large sums of money that are given to us they assume that our treasury is overflowing. We have never been rich or even close to it. There was no way that we could afford a $500,000 Center or a $175,000 home for women or any of the other buildings we have. God, though, has given us a boldness to go forward: when we sense that He is leading us, we go, no matter how hard our teeth may be chattering and our knees knocking. Once we have plunged headfirst into ventures of this sort, God has always intervened and has motivated people to bail us out. It is not our intention to make ourselves into beggars, nor do we wish to get so far into debt that people will give to us out of sympathy. Prayer-led, we have gone forward. God-inspired, men have come to our rescue.

It has been our experience that it is more important to stop to consider Christ than the cost. Those who have not witnessed miraculous answers to prayers of this type find it difficult to believe this. I thought my faith was strong, yet I sometimes realized that I was lying awake until the early hours of the morning because I was worried about how we were going to meet our bills. I am embarrassed to admit that, for it was an indication that I felt that all the responsibilities rested on me and that if I did not figure out some way of raising money fast we would not survive. Now I know that this is the job of the Lord, who has promised to take care of our every need.

Teen Challenge is officially connected with the Assemblies of God churches and our board of directors is made up mainly of ministers from this denomination. Nevertheless, we strive to keep an interdenominational image. We allow people going through our program to attend services at churches of various denominations, and, as far as finances go, about 85 percent of all our contributions come from outside the Assemblies of God. Yes, we have done a lot of praying about finances at Teen Challenge, but we have also prayed mightily that the Lord would make us wise stewards of the funds that come our way.

When I look back at the way in which some of this money has come to us, I shake my head in wonderment. In September of 1964 we were on the brink of being penniless. Each day

we kept paying out more money than we received. Dave said
in chapel one day that he felt that on the following Tuesday
we would receive a check that would take care of our needs.
Our needs were substantial, so that meant that the check
would have to be substantial. Since it was on a Thursday that
Dave had made this prediction, we had to wait five days to see
if it would be fulfilled. In Tuesday's mail there came a check
from a woman in Pittsburgh. It was for $10,000.

Why do we go through such periods of financial stress?
Well, I think one of the reasons is that it is the Lord's way
of showing us that He still answers prayers. Another reason
is that the dramatic answers to our needs have helped to
strengthen the faith of Christians everywhere, especially those
in our program. I wish that everyone could see the joy on the
faces of people around the Center when they get news that
weeks of prayer about our latest need have been answered.
News such as this travels fast. When people get the good report,
they respond in different ways: some fall on their knees and
thank God, others raise their eyes heavenward and shout out
a prayer, and some, overcome with joy, sit down and weep.

One reason we have had so many financial crises is because
of the size of our budget. Our daily expenses average close to
$1,000. Even with all the free food and cut-rate prices that we
get, our cost for meals is more than $3,000 a month. Utilities
cost an average of nearly $2,000 a month and we are still paying
$2,100 a month for the Teen Challenge Institute of Missions.
Postage for a month costs some $500. There have been oc-
casions when we have had to scrape together every nickel,
dime and penny that we could find in order to buy food. Yet,
as close as we have come to the bottom of the financial barrel,
we have never gone without eating. At Teen Challenge we
have an expression that goes like this: "We live from hand to
mouth—from God's hand to our mouth."

Our needs have been taken care of in some extraordinary
ways. A fairly well-to-do businessman came all the way from
Ceylon to Clinton Avenue. When he arrived in Brooklyn he
told me that he wanted to spend some time with us so that he
could learn about our workings and then return to Ceylon to
set up a ministry comparable to ours. "God has told me to live

by faith, so that's what I plan to do," he said, as he turned over to me all his money except for six dollars, which he kept to take care of his immediate needs. After spending two months with us, he returned to Ceylon, sold his business, and set up his ministry.

A young man named Freddy Ramirez stopped in to see Dave one day. Freddy, who lives in The Bronx, explained that he had recently been discharged from the Armed Forces and that while he had been in Vietnam he and other soldiers had read about our work. They had asked their chaplain to designate a portion of their contributions to our support, Freddy explained, whereupon he handed Dave a check on behalf of himself and his comrades for $611.60.

Two of our most unusual donations have come from a sports fan and a professional football player. Enclosed with one check was a note saying, "I have heard about your wonderful work and want to do something. Therefore, I am enclosing a check for $13—my winnings from the race track today. I am pledging other future winnings also." His next check was for $40. On another occasion, we received a check for $200 from the New York Jets football team. It wasn't until a few months later that I found out that the money had actually come from Dainard Paulson, one of the Jet players. Paulson had been fined $200 by the Jets for some infraction, but under club policy the player can have the money turned over to any charity he desires and Dainard selected us.

One woman who had heard about our ministry called our business manager in the middle of the night to tell him how impressed she was. "I'm coming right over there to work with you people," she said. Our business manager tried to explain that we didn't hire workers in such a manner. She remained firm, though, and insisted that she would be over the next day to begin working. Sure enough, the next day she was at the Center.

I was informed about the situation and consented to speak to her. It didn't take long to determine that she had problems of her own, but I was able to convince her that before she could enter a type of work that was designed to help other people she would first have to help herself get well. She had emotional difficulties, was a chain smoker, and was highly nervous. She said that she would gladly stay to undergo treatment, but, after three days, during which time she did a lot of complaining, she left. Theo Edwards, one of the girls on our staff, though, had been able to get through to her, and before this woman left she had accepted the Lord. After she left, she wrote a letter to Theo, thanked her for her help and sent along a check for $6,000. We had doubts about how good that check might be, so we phoned the bank in Charlotte, North Carolina, where this woman had her account. "Don't worry about her," the bank executive told us. "Her father is independently wealthy and she has a trust fund. That check is all right." About a year after that I met this woman at a gospel meeting in Brooklyn. I didn't recognize her at first. She had lost weight, her face was more radiant, and she was a more relaxed and confident person now that she was living for the Lord.

One day at our farm in Pennsylvania a man wearing work clothes drove up in a jeep. After asking Reverend Frank Reynolds if he could show him around, he was given a tour of the grounds. As he was leaving, the man said, "I'd like to have my wife come look at this place." Then off he drove.

A few weeks later, a helicopter hovered over the farm, then landed. Out stepped the man who had come in the jeep to look the place over. This time his wife was with him. They took a trip around the farm and then departed. Not long afterward, Reverend Reynolds received a telephone call from this man, who turned out to be the president of a large chemical plant in Philadelphia. "I want to help you," he began, "so I'm going to send you some stocks. They are worth $6,700 and I would advise you to sell them right away before the value goes down." We weren't able to sell the stocks immediately, but when we did the value had gone up, not down, and we were able to get $7,100 for them.

One of the worst financial droughts we ever experienced was the one that occurred in the summer of 1967. Day after day, our income just dribbled in. At the end of each day we were deeper in debt than when we had started. We started a prayer chain at the Center with everyone asking the Lord to help us meet our budget. Finally, we got to the point where things began to look really bleak. We owed a total of $15,000. I passed the word around for everyone to pray for a specific amount: $15,000. A few days later, we received a check for $1,000 and we rejoiced about that. Still, we were $14,000 short, and if we didn't have the money by Monday morning we would be in bad shape. We had received grants worth more than $14,000, but never had we had a check for such a sum. This was the first real financial crisis since I had taken over as director of the Center and I began to get edgy. On Saturday morning, July 24, I went to my office and fished through the mail. Nothing looked promising. Slowly, I opened one envelope after the other. There were plenty of bills, but not much else. I looked at the stack of mail and saw that there were only a few envelopes left. The first contained another bill. In the next one there was a check. I looked at the signature. Never heard of the man, I thought to myself. Then I looked at the figures written on the check. My hands began to tremble. I stared at the check and then called out to my wife, who was in the office with me, "Look. Look at this. Can you believe it?" Then I noticed the letter that had come with the check. It read: "I was praying and God impressed upon my heart that I should send you a check for $14,000."

seventeen /...

···/ the tragedy and
/ the triumph

MAINLINING TWO, THREE, FOUR, a dozen times a day, an addict gets so high that the world looks like cotton candy and reality takes on the texture of peach fuzz. It's like, man, there ain't nothing—no worries, no time, zero. And that, sadly, is the verdict of *all* addicts. Why do they do it? It is a haunting question. They do it because they know that life—if it is to make sense, if it is to be worth living—must have a deeper meaning than they are experiencing. Of the thousands of addicts who have come to Teen Challenge, however, not a single one has ever told us that he had found that deeper meaning through dope or that drugs had given him the happiness, kicks or thrills that he had sought. What's more, never have I heard of anyone anywhere who was happy that he had become addicted.

It all begins so innocently: a friend offers you a drag on a marijuana cigarette, another buddy invites you to a pot party, a pusher hands you several bags of heroin so you can try it and see how you like it. He explains that these bags are free; later there is a fee for your drugs—your life. You can take your yellowish-white powdery heroin out of its glassine bag and snort it (sniff it) or inject yourself with it without hitting a vein. Both methods will keep you from getting too much of a jolt too fast. If you want to go big-time, though, you mainline it. This process of injecting yourself is complicated at first. But before you know it, you're pouring that heroin into the empty cap of a wine bottle without spilling a fleck of it and you don't even have to look to properly jam the bottle cap into the V formed by spreading a bobby pin apart. You may have a hard time keeping down the shakes as you hold first one match and then a second under your bottle-cap cooker, but you know that you will soon evaporate into your own special world of zero. Now that the heroin has been liquefied, you carefully draw the fluid into a hypodermic needle. Before the cooking had begun, you had tied a handkerchief, belt or rope around your upper arm to force a blood vessel to bulge so that it would be an easy target for your needle. Now the needle and the vein are both ready. A moment to aim, a moment to shoot the heroin into the vein—then you lie back and wait for the drowsy timelessness to take you away. And when it's all over, you're right back where you started from.

You're not quite certain what happened. One thing you know, though, is that you're smarter than those other guys, too smart ever to get hooked. Your veins, why are they collapsing? How much weight have you lost? Why can't you sleep? Where did all those body sores come from? You know it's happening, but you're too smart, aren't you? Or aren't you smart enough? Okay, so you're hooked. You know you can kick it any time you want to. So you stay off stuff for a couple days. Then you go back on H, only now it's seven, eight times a day instead of three or four. Who can you rob next to get the money for your drugs? Why is life becoming so frantic? Police. Detention homes. Parole officers. Jails. Hospitals. Everybody's against you. Doesn't anybody care? Can't somebody help you before you die?

There are a hundred thousand such addicts in New York City—all the same, yet no two alike. Many cling to life only because they fear death. Others, devoid of a purpose to live for and unable to tolerate the cursedness of their existence, choose death because they feel it cannot be worse than life. I recall a girl who went up on the rooftop of a Brooklyn building on a sunny summer's day and injected herself with an overdose of heroin. She died. Her body was not found until eight days later. No one had missed her. No one mourned her. I heard a sixteen-year-old boy curse the day he had been born and I saw an even younger girl—once pretty, perhaps, but now living in a bleached-out body—plead for death as her only hope.

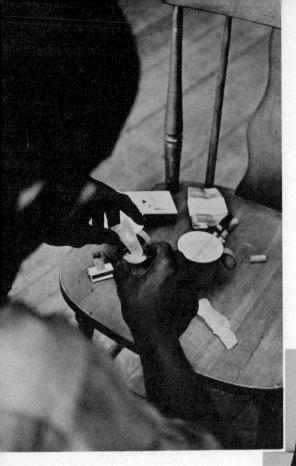

"Mainlining it" . . .

Above: Drug addict prepares to "shoot up," a daily ritual that takes him into a chemical heaven. *Right:* Ready to "drill" into vein for a heroin "high."

Whenever possible, we prefer working with youngsters because if we can clean them of drugs it will spare them long years of torment. Unfortunately, teenagers often turn their backs on us. They have not been on what we call the "misery-go-round" long enough, have not had enough difficulties, beatings, jail sentences, scares and pain to make them desperate enough to see their need. It hurts to see a young boy or girl walk away from Teen Challenge and know that all he or she needs to be ready for our program is a few more years filled with fear, of running from the law, of stealing, hiding and living on the fringe of oblivion. Until every moment becomes fraught with an almost paralyzing futility, they are seldom prepared to come to us with a hope that is carved out of desperation.

Youngsters often steer away from Christianity because, presented incorrectly, what they see of it is unappealing. They see lukewarm Christians plodding on from day to day and that repels them. I like the way Dave spoke up about this situation. He said, "Kids are tired of 'bless-me clubs' that pass as churches. They want a church that is alive and active, not cold and dead." Just how alive and active true Christianity can be is hard for the non-believer to comprehend. Our work at Teen Challenge has helped to portray Christianity in action. One of the most rewarding aspects of our work has been that large numbers of the people who go through our program have active Christian lives. Many are pastors and those who are not in full-time service are Christians-on-the-go, men and women who are vibrant. Real Christianity does not spawn lazy people.

No one can tell me that Christianity has to be cold and dead or that it has to be a joke. Hundreds of times I have seen some of the most desperate men and women transformed through the power of Christ. I have seen men who have had lives that were as thrill-packed as one could ever imagine— lives filled with knives and bullets and police sirens; and I have heard these same men say that the most exciting thing that has ever happened to them has been their acceptance of Christ. I have heard them tell me that the excitement has not tapered off and that the everyday lives they lead as Christians are packed with far more action than any they had ever known before.

One of our most successful means of presenting Christ to men has been by distributing thousands of tracts and booklets. Perhaps the most effective piece of literature we have put out ourselves is a tract called *Chicken,* which was written by Dave in 1960 and updated by me in 1967. The title itself has provoked various responses. One girl looked at the title, then said, "My mother already has a good recipe for chicken." A young boy asked me, "What does this title mean?" When I told him, "It means that you're chicken if you don't read it," he snapped back, "Then let me read it right now."

I saw a man wandering aimlessly around Clinton Avenue one afternoon; when I asked if I could assist him he reached into his pocket, pulled out a copy of *Chicken* and pointed to the address of Teen Challenge on the back page. Angel Ingles, who was so high on drugs that he couldn't find Teen Challenge even though he was standing right in front of it, was in bad shape when he came to us that day. He admitted that he had been using drugs for years and that now, nine months after he had been given a copy of our tract, he knew that he had to turn to God for help. With drugs out of his life and with Christ in his heart, Angel now runs a grocery store and restaurant on Long Island and has done extensive work to help Spanish-speaking folks find the same joy that he now has.

A copy of *Chicken* was picked up by a girl while she was in a phone booth placing a call. Curiosity, more than anything else, prompted her to put it in her pocketbook. She was a college girl and an agnostic and it was not because of any interest in God that she read the tract when she got home. She read it because, well, because when she opened her pocketbook there it was. As she read it, though, she began to understand her need for Christ. She came to Teen Challenge, gave up narcotics, and accepted salvation through Jesus Christ. She dropped out of college, went to Bible school, and is now a full-time servant of the Lord. I'll always wonder what would have happened if she had not gone to the right phone booth on the right day to make that call.

Scores of people have told us that they carried copies of

Chicken or other pieces of our literature for months and, in some instances, for years. Instinctively, they realized that these tracts contained the answer they sought. When I asked one man why he had come to Teen Challenge, he showed me a well-worn copy of *Chicken,* then explained that he had kept it with him at all times so that he would always have our address available "just in case."

Unfortunately, not even the power of the written word can penetrate the hearts of some men. When one of our staffers heard about an old friend's involvements in homosexuality he sent him two copies of a booklet of ours, *Hope for the Homosexual.* Here is a copy of the letter that the man on our staff received in return:

"I received the Teen Challenge letter this morning with the two copies of *Hope for the Homosexual* in it. I immediately read one copy and I think it is very good and does provide the only cure for homosexuality. However, words are not enough. We gay people need someone to love us and someone to understand us and to talk with us. I know God loves us, and He understands us, and we can talk to Him, but I mean a real person here on earth for us to go to. Someone who will not ridicule or scorn us.

"I suppose you know that I am completely homosexual now and that I have degraded to the point now where I am nothing but a cheap and immoral person. I engage in all the practices that any homosexual could possibly engage in. I walk the streets late at night, go to gay bars and theaters and linger in restrooms waiting to make my contacts for the night. I pick up about ten dollars a night now from businessmen in town who cannot afford to be open about their problem. My life is a complete mess.

"But don't let me make you think I am happy. I'm not. I'm miserable and looking for a way out. We who are hooked will be queer for the rest of our lives. Sure, I'm miserable and frustrated and tormented. I've even had a nervous breakdown and am possibly facing another. God speaks to me, but I have to push Him out of my life.

"Thanks for the books and your concern, but sadly and

unfortunately there is no hope for me any more. I don't want to go to hell, but there's not much that can be done to correct my situation now. I will pass the books on to some of my gay friends and maybe they can find a way out if they want to do so. Once again, thanks for taking the time to send them to me and for your concern and interest in my life."

A policeman called one night to say that the body of a teenage boy had been found and that he was hoping we might be able to provide some identification. He explained that the boy had carried no identification and that the only thing in his pockets was a card which said, "If you are a drug addict and need help, call this number at Teen Challenge immediately."

One of the men who returned to us via a circuitous route that took him to jail on Riker's Island, brought back with him a copy of a poem written by an addict he had met while behind bars.

I AM
A NUMBER

Time
   measured by an empty room
      between heartbeats and paper prayers
Or through a dusty window
     the light seen
    kissing particles and sliding down the wall
       to trip over a picture
       of trees and grass
   and fall sprawling across the bones of an old wooden chair
     splashing the floor with forgotten warmth
   and surprising the roaches playing king of the mountain
      on yesterday's paper
   and finally creeping across the dresser
    to bathe in a glass of bloody water
       next to an eye dropper
       and a needle
  two glassine bags
    torn and empty
  and the bottle top
     still containing traces of yesterday's hope.
There is no more.
The door is locked
    the bed is cold
      and i am a number.

If only men could understand that in God's sight they are not mere numbers but His children whom He wants to hold close and give all the love and help they need.

Because it is so hard to get some people to Teen Challenge, there is much rejoicing for each one who goes through our program. One such man, who had been a pimp and a pusher, who had been arrested twenty-three times and had served fourteen years in prison, became the president of his class in Bible school after graduating from our Center. Now there are the LSD users, most of them better educated than the drug addicts. One of them, a dean's list student in college, came to us from Minnesota. He stood up in chapel and addressed himself to the other men one day, saying, "I want you to know how much all of you mean to me. I've been tempted to leave here and go home, but I look around at you and realize that all you have to do to go home or back where you can get drugs is to walk outside and get a subway. I want to thank you for the courage you've given me to believe that I can make it here." He made it all right and is now working as a field representative for us.

We may be short on funds, but as long as we remain long on prayer I know that we will survive. After our disappointing attempt to relocate our Center on Staten Island we felt certain that it was the Lord who had intervened. Although neither Dave nor I could fathom why we were not supposed to build on Staten Island, we both believed that we would some day have our answer. It was a long time coming. When it did, we thanked God for *not* letting us build on Staten Island. Had we built on the site where we had wanted to we would have a funny-looking Center; at least I think it would be, since it would have a four-lane highway going right through the front door.

So often the Lord works in ways like this, causing things to occur that none of us can explain at the moment. During one of our worst financial crises we reached the point where we didn't have money to buy our next meal. I explained this to the men at our morning chapel service and told them to pray for thirty-five dollars, which was what it would cost to buy provisions for lunch. One after another they prayed fervently, and after twenty minutes or so I heard a tapping sound at the rear of the chapel. When I looked up I saw a woman softly knocking on the door, which was open. I walked back and asked if I could be of help to her.

"I don't know," she said. "I'm not sure why I'm here. It's just that I got this feeling that I should come over right away. Something was telling me to take the money out of a piggy bank I've been putting change into and that I should bring it here. I couldn't get rid of the thought, so I figured I'd better come over."

She handed me a brown paper bag containing the coins she had spoken of. Then she left. We counted the money at once. It came to $35.50. As for the woman, I had never seen her before and I've never seen her since.

During an evening chapel service an addict stood up and said, "I can't believe this place. No bars on the windows. No guards. All these guys are drug addicts and they aren't even trying to break out. They're staying on their own. Never heard of anything like it. Do you think that something like this can happen to me?" It can happen and it did happen to that man, who committed his life to Christ and was able to free himself of drugs.

So many wonderful things have happened to us that we have to be cautious not to become immune to the miraculous way in which the Lord works, no matter how often we witness it. This is a point I have tried to get across to our workers, telling them that we live amid the extraordinary at Teen Challenge and that we must never let it turn into the ordinary. This is very difficult; even God's chosen people became so accustomed to God's miracles that they shrugged them off. To avoid this we must always set new goals, must undertake new burdens so that we will remain vigorous in our work and our outlook. I remind our workers that because the victories are greater, in a sense, in the sort of work we do, that we must be aware that the setbacks will be proportionately as great.

A major reason why Teen Challenge has moved forward is because we have been blessed with a fine group of workers, people who have been dedicated to their jobs and who have done them well. Cookie Rivera explained her ability to prosper in the work by saying, "The Lord gave me unction for my

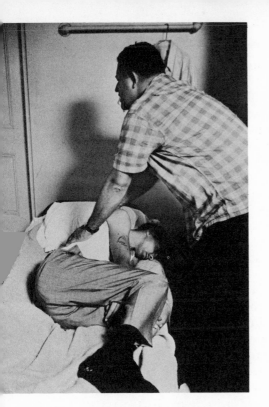

Left: Converted addict prays for newly admitted "junkie."
Below: Don Wilkerson interviews converted addict in chapel.

gumption so that I could function." Still, it is a demanding, oftentimes frustrating work. One staff worker used to say, "I just don't fit in around here. I'm resigning." At times like that I would say, "Don't be upset. I resign every Monday morning." They don't quit, though. Instead, they work harder. When one saw a convert in need of a coat, he gave him his own. And when that same worker had worn holes in the soles of his shoes, a stranger pressed an envelope into his hand. Inside was fifteen dollars and a note saying, "All God's children got shoes."

Today, we house as many as thirty-five addicts at 416. All in all, we constantly work with between 175 and 200 men, women and children in all phases of our ministry, from the Center to the farm, from the school to the children's home, from the girls' home through our re-entry program.

We have had almost-dead people come to us and have watched them return to society with something worth living for. Having seen lives transformed in this way, we press on in the hope that all drug addicts and all troubled men will find similar joy through Christ Jesus. I have yet to meet anyone—school teacher, bank president, truck driver, housewife, student—who has found complete happiness and satisfaction without first having found Christ.

Whenever someone asks why we have established our ministry in such a tumultuous area, I explain how the Lord simply wouldn't let us go elsewhere. I also like to think of the words of C. T. Studd, a missionary who wrote:

> Some want to live within the sound
> Of church or chapel bell;
> I want to run a rescue shop
> Within a yard of hell.

There is a need for our ministry right where it is. I think that one of the best reasons any of our converts ever gave for coming to Teen Challenge was, as he put it, "because I've felt the power of the devil all my life and I *knew* there had to be another power on the other side." If we were not on that "other side," a lot of people would be looking in vain.

Another addict told me, "Your Christianity is all right for

kids and old ladies, but it won't work out here in the gutter and the ghetto." Well, Christianity has worked because we have brought it to precisely those two places: the gutter and the ghetto. We have stooped down to the gutter and we have labored in the ghetto. And we have looked at the wretched people there, lifting them up, showing them Christ, and praying with them for a new life, one with meaning and love. The first time you reach down to the gutter and put your hands on a crusty alcoholic or dope addict who is caked with filth, the first time you bend down and your nostrils are filled with the stench that has been his for so long, the first time you are not certain whether the body you are lifting is dead or alive— that's when you realize there isn't a thing that *you* can do for him and that you must commit this man to God in prayer. To see such a man as this months later as he walks out of Teen Challenge with Bible in hand makes me pause to thank God for what He has wrought.